I0809872

LifeLight™
FOUNDATIONS

"In Him was life, and the life was the light of men." John 1:4

End Times

LEADERS GUIDE

CONCORDIA PUBLISHING HOUSE • SAINT LOUIS

Hans Memling's *Last Judgment* (ca. 1467–71; found in the National Museum in Gdansk, Poland) focuses on the calling of Jesus Christ, who will judge the world on the Last Day (cf. Revelation 4:2–3). The sword extending from Jesus' mouth represents God's word of condemnation to those who reject the Lord and His ways (Revelation 19:15). The lily represents God's word of grace to those trusting in the Lord, who will share in His resurrection. As you study the end times, note how the Scriptures clearly teach both messages while emphasizing God's willing grace for all people (1 Timothy 2:4).

3558 S. Jefferson Ave., St. Louis, MO 63118-3968
1-800-325-3040 • www.cph.org

Written by Cameron MacKenzie

Edited by Brian Chisamore

Cover: *Last Judgment* (detail), by Hans Memling. SuperStock/SuperStock

This publication may be available in Braille, in large print, or on cassette tape for the visually impaired. Please allow 8 to 12 weeks for delivery. Write to Lutheran Braille Workers, P.O. Box 5000, Yucaipa, CA 92399; call toll-free 1-800-925-6092; or visit the Web site: www.LBWinc.org.

Manufactured in the United States of America

1 2 3 4 5 6 7 8 9 10 23 22 21 20 19 18 17 16 15 14

Contents

Introduction

Welcome to LifeLight

A special pleasure is in store for you. You will be instrumental in leading your brothers and sisters in Christ closer to Him who is our life and light (John 1:4). You will have the pleasure of seeing fellow Christians discover new insights and rediscover old ones as they open the Scriptures and dig deep into them, perhaps deeper than they have ever dug before. More than that, you will have the pleasure of sharing in this wonderful study.

LifeLight—An In-depth Study

LifeLight is a series of in-depth Bible studies. The goal of LifeLight is that through a regular program of in-depth personal and group study of Scripture, more and more Christian adults may grow in their personal faith in Jesus Christ, enjoy fellowship with the members of His body, and reach out in love to others in witness and service.

In-depth means that this Bible study includes the following four components: individual daily home study; discussion in a small group; a lecture presentation on the Scripture portion under study; and an enhancement of the week's material (through reading the enrichment magazine).

LifeLight Participants

LifeLight participants are adults who desire a deeper study of the Scriptures than is available in the typical Sunday morning adult Bible class. (Mid-to-older teens might also be LifeLight participants.) While LifeLight does not assume an existing knowledge of the Bible or special experience or skills in Bible study, it does assume a level of commitment that will bring participants to each of the nine weekly assemblies having read the assigned readings and attempted to answer the study questions. Daily reading and study will require from 15 to 30 minutes for the five days preceding the LifeLight assembly. The day following the assembly will be spent reviewing the previous week's study by going over the completed study leaflet and the enrichment magazine.

LifeLight Leadership

While the in-depth process used by LifeLight begins with individual study and cannot achieve its aims without this individual effort, it cannot be completed by individual study alone. Therefore, trained leaders are necessary. You fill one or perhaps more of the important roles described below.

The Director

This person oversees the LifeLight program in a local center (which may be a congregation or a center operated by several neighboring congregations). The director

- serves as the parish LifeLight overall coordinator and leader;
- coordinates the scheduling of the LifeLight program;
- orders materials;
- convenes LifeLight leadership-team meetings;
- develops publicity materials;
- recruits participants;
- maintains records and budgeting;
- assigns, with the leadership team, participants to small discussion groups;
- makes arrangements for facilities;
- communicates outreach opportunities to small-group leaders and to congregational boards;
- follows up on participants who leave the program.

The Assistant Director *(optional)*

This person may assist the director. Duties listed for the director may be assigned to the assistant director as mutually agreeable.

The Lecture Leader

This person prepares and delivers the lecture at the weekly assembly. **(Lesson material for the lecture leader begins on p. 9.)** The lecture leader

- prepares and presents the Bible study lecture to the large group;

- prepares worship activities (devotional thought, hymn, prayer), using resources in the study leaflet and leaders guide and possibly other, outside sources;
- helps the small-group discussion leaders to grow in understanding the content of the lessons;
- encourages prayer at weekly leadership team and discussion leaders meetings.

The Small-Group Coordinator *(optional; the director may fill this role)*

This person supervises and coordinates the work of the small-group discussion leaders. The small-group coordinator

- recruits with the leadership team the small-group discussion leaders;
- trains or arranges for training of the discussion leaders;
- assists the director and discussion leaders in follow-up and outreach;
- encourages the discussion leaders to contact absent group members;
- participates in the weekly leadership-team and discussion-leaders equipping meetings;
- provides ongoing training and support as needed.

The Small-Group Discussion Leaders

These people guide and facilitate discussion of LifeLight participants in the small groups. **(Lesson material for the small-group leaders begins on p. 57.)** There should be one discussion leader for every group of no more than twelve participants. The small-group discussion leaders are, perhaps, those individuals who are most important to the success of the program. They should, therefore, be chosen with special care and be equipped with skills needed to guide discussion and to foster a caring fellowship within the group. These discussion leaders

- prepare each week for the small-group discussion by using the study leaflet and small-group leaders guide section for that session **(see p. 55)**;
- read the enrichment magazine as a study supplement;
- guide and facilitate discussion in their small group;
- encourage and assist the discussion group in prayer;
- foster fellowship and mutual care within the discussion group;
- attend weekly discussion leaders training meetings.

Leadership Training

LifeLight leaders will meet weekly to review the previous week's work and plan the coming week. At this session, leaders can address concerns and prepare for the coming session. LifeLight is a 1½-hour program with no possibility for it to be taught in the one hour typically available on Sunday mornings. Some congregations, however, may want to use the Sunday morning Bible study hour for LifeLight preparation and leadership training. In such a meeting, the lecture leader and/or small-group coordinator may lead the discussion leaders through the coming week's lesson, reserving 5 or 10 minutes for problem solving or other group concerns.

While it requires intense effort, LifeLight has proven to bring great benefit to LifeLight participants. The effort put into this program, both by leaders and by participants, will be rewarding and profitable.

The LifeLight Weekly Schedule

Here is how LifeLight will work week by week:

1. Before session 1, each participant will receive the study leaflet for session 1 and the enrichment magazine for the course. The study leaflet contains worship resources (for use both in individual daily study and at the opening of the following week's assembly) and readings and study questions for five days. Challenge questions will lead those participants who have the time and desire a greater challenge into even deeper levels of study.

2. After the five days of individual study at home, participants will gather for a weekly assembly of all LifeLight participants. The assembly will begin with a brief period of worship (5 minutes). Participants will then join their assigned small discussion groups (of twelve or fewer, who will remain the same throughout the course), where they will go over the week's study questions together (55 minutes). Assembling together once again, participants will listen to a lecture presentation on the readings they have studied in the previous week and discussed in their small groups (20 minutes). After the lecture presentation, the director or another leader will distribute the study leaflet for the following week. Closing announcements and other necessary business may take another five minutes before dismissal.

In some places some small groups will not join the weekly assembly because of scheduling or other reasons. Such groups may meet at another time and place (perhaps in the home of one of the small group's members). Those congregations may record the lecture given by the lecture leader at the weekly assembly and duplicate it for use by other groups meeting later in the week.

3. On the day following the assembly, participants will review the preceding week's work by rereading the study leaflet they completed (and that they perhaps supplemented or corrected during the discussion in their small group) and by reading appropriate articles in the enrichment magazine.

Then, the LifeLight weekly study process will begin all over again!

Recommended Resources for Study and Worship

The Lutheran Study Bible. St. Louis: Concordia Publishing House, 2009. This resource contains more than 26,000 study and application notes, a most thorough reference guide (pp. lxv–cx), and over 90,000 cross-references, as well as a 31,000-entry concordance, maps, charts, and timelines.

Roehrs, Walter R., and Martin H. Franzmann. *Concordia Self-Study Commentary.* St. Louis: Concordia Publishing House, 1979. This one-volume commentary on the Bible contains 950 pages and is tailored for lay use.

The Concordia Organist is a 31-CD collection of pipe organ accompaniments for all the hymns and liturgical music in *Lutheran Service Book*. St. Louis: Concordia Publishing House (order no. 99-2264). Use these CDs for worship hymn accompaniment.

Last Things

Matthew 3:2, 11–12

Preparing for the Session

Central Focus

The main purpose of this lecture is to offer reasons for a study of the end times. Students will learn that the second coming of Jesus (along with the resurrection and judgment) are essential elements in the Christian religion—elements that offer great motivation for Christian living and great comfort in Christian dying. Students will also learn that the Bible has a great deal to say about the end times. This theme is a vital part of the Christian religion.

Objectives

That participants, led by the Holy Spirit working through God's Word, will

1. realize how important are God's promises about the last things;
2. learn that teachings about the last things are pervasive in the New Testament; and
3. prepare for the end in view of what God has revealed.

Note for the small-group leaders: Lesson notes and other materials you will need begin on page 57.

For the Lecture Leader

Session Plan

Worship

Begin the session with the hymn printed in the study leaflet. Accompaniments are available in denominational hymnals, such as *Lutheran Service Book* or *Lutheran Worship* (refer to hymnal index). (Note: Concordia Publishing House has available *The Concordia Organist.* All the initial worship hymns in the LifeLight courses are included in this resource. It's especially helpful for mission congregations and small parishes. See the list of study resources on page 7.) Follow with this prayer:

Prayer

Heavenly Father, as we begin this study of the end times, we pray for the Holy Spirit to enlighten our minds that we may understand what You have revealed about the last things and to comfort our hearts with Your promises of resurrection and life everlasting; through Jesus Christ our Lord. Amen.

Lecture Presentation

1 Introduction

Aristotle once wrote that a good drama has a beginning, a middle, and an end, and most of us would agree that such organization is helpful. Whether we're watching a play or a television show, or just reading a novel, we want things to make sense. An author cannot assume that his readers know what's going on before he tells them, and he shouldn't leave them with a lot of questions when he finishes. And, of course, something interesting has to take place between the first and last lines. Otherwise, the story fails. The writing may be excellent, but the story is not. It makes no sense.

To many people in the modern world, the story of humanity is a literary failure. It has a middle for sure, and a vague sort of beginning, but certainly no end—at least, not one that wraps up all the loose ends. Each individual life certainly comes to a conclusion. But what about the whole thing? Is humanity doomed just to muddle along as it has in the past? Or is there a goal, a final reckoning, an ending that makes sense?

Of course, not every story "makes sense" in the same way. Some leave us laughing and others weeping. Good often triumphs, but not always. In human history—fact, not fiction—evil sometimes wins, perhaps more often than not. We like to think that history is going somewhere good. Maybe this is even true from a technological and scientific standpoint, but what about social arrangements or even common morality? A major result of the Internet has been easy access to pornography. Is that good? Medical science has made it convenient to terminate a just-conceived human life with a pill. Is that good? Nations around the world have changed their legal systems to accommodate and affirm homosexual relationships. Is that good?

Obviously, no. History may be going somewhere, but we can't always call it progress. So where is the world really going and how will it all end? The purpose of this course is to study the ending—the real one taught by the Bible.

2 Christians Confess the End

So this is where the Christian religion comes in. We believe not only that the world had a beginning (Creation) and a (glorious) middle (our Lord's death and resurrection), but that it will also have an end. For, as we confess in the Creed, "He will come to judge the living and the dead."

Unfortunately, many of us find this hard to believe. Like the scoffers to whom Peter once referred, we ask, (2 Peter 3:4) "Where is the promise of His coming? For ever since the fathers fell asleep, all things are continuing as they were from the beginning of creation." Day after day, year after year, generation after generation, the world goes on as it has in the past. The narratives of the Bible may inspire us, and the truths of our faith may encourage us, but we still find ourselves longing for the promised ending—the resurrection of the body and the life everlasting. Without it, even the Christian "story" makes no sense.

In his First Epistle to the Corinthians, Paul wrote: (15:19) "If in Christ we have hope in this life only, we are of all people most to be pitied." Paul knew that only the promised resurrection at the end of time would bring the fulfillment of everything that our Lord had accomplished through His own death and resurrection. Then and then only, would sin and death—the great plagues of human existence—be gone forever. Short of that, sin and death would remain in charge. The devil would remain in charge. So what kind of hope is there without an ending? None at all.

But Christians live by hope. God promises life, but all we see is death. God promises forgiveness, but all we experience is sin. So we must hope for the fulfillment of all that God has promised. Our faith means both "now" and "not yet." God's Word is good, and He doesn't lie. By Baptism and faith, we are the children of God; we are the heirs of all that God promises. There can be no doubt about it. Nevertheless, "now we see in a mirror dimly" (1 Corinthians 13:12), and we do not yet fully experience the blessings that God has bestowed. Hunger, thirst, heat, and tears remain the lot of every person, every Christian here, but God promises: (Revelation 7:16–17)

> They shall hunger no more, neither thirst anymore;
> the sun shall not strike them,
> nor any scorching heat.
> For the Lamb in the midst of the throne will be their shepherd,
> and He will guide them to springs of living water,
> and God will wipe away every tear from their eyes.

So the Christian confession of the "end" is an essential element of our faith. God promises it, and we want it desperately. The Gospel is empty without it.

But if that's the case, then why does God delay? One answer, of course, is that God's ways are not our ways. He is in charge, and we are not in charge; and in our better moments, we all have to acknowledge that that is certainly for the best. We must simply trust in God our heavenly Father to do what is good and right for His people.

But in this particular instance—the timing of the end—God has revealed to us His motive for delay ("delay" only from our point of view, not His). In response to scoffers who question whether Jesus is coming back at all, Peter assured the faithful: (2 Peter 3:9) "The Lord is not slow to fulfill His promise as some count slowness, but is patient toward you, not wishing that any should perish but that all should reach repentance." God is not a creature of time; He is its Lord. He uses time to accomplish His purposes—His good and gracious purposes—in this case, time for the Word of the Gospel to go out and summon all men to repentance.

Our Lord Himself has told us: (Matthew 24:14) "This gospel of the kingdom will be proclaimed throughout the whole world as a testimony to all nations, and then the end will come." In Matthew 28, Jesus outlined the Church's task and history: (v. 19) "Go therefore and make disciples of all nations." Only when that task has been completed—only when the last possible person has been gathered in—only then will the end come. The sole reason for God's "delay" is God's grace, His love for lost sinners who need to hear the Gospel before the Last Day.

3 Jesus and the End Times

Statements about the end are pervasive in the New Testament, beginning with the Gospels. In fact, in the very first Gospel, when John the Baptist began to preach, he announced, (Matthew 3:2) "Repent, for the kingdom of heaven is at hand," and then elaborated, (vv. 11–12) "He who is coming after me is mightier than I. . . . He will baptize you with the Holy Spirit and fire. His winnowing fork is in his hand, and He will clear His threshing floor and gather His wheat into the barn, but the chaff He will burn with *unquenchable fire* [emphasis mine]." Right from the outset, therefore, the New Testament sounds the motif of judgment in connection with Christ's work.

Of course, in the Scriptures, the "kingdom" that John announced means more than just Judgment Day. First and foremost, the kingdom of heaven (or of God) refers to the new relationship with God that Jesus not only preached but also creates. After all, He is "God with us" (Matthew 1:23). Therefore, from His assault upon Satan's rule by casting out demons, we should realize that "the kingdom of God has come upon you" (Matthew 12:28) and that He can even say to the Pharisees who wanted to know when the Kingdom would come, "The kingdom of God is in the midst of you" (Luke 17:21). After all, Jesus was right there in front of them!

However, there are many, many passages in which the theme of judgment and the end are prominent aspects of the kingdom of God. Just think, for example, of some of the well-known "Kingdom" parables, like that of the wedding feast (Matthew 22:1–14) or of the ten virgins (Matthew 25:1–13). Both begin with statements comparing the kingdom of heaven to the main themes of the story, a wedding feast in the one and maidens waiting for the bridegroom in the other. Both conclude with pictures of judgment. In the first case, a man without a wedding garment is cast into outer darkness, and in the second, the foolish virgins cannot get into the feast. In each parable, the meaning includes being ready for the end.

Jesus also spoke of the end very directly, not just in parables. Already in the Sermon on the Mount, He included what some have called "the little judgment scene": (Matthew 7:21, 23) "On that day many will say to Me. . . . And then will I declare to them, 'I never knew you; depart from Me, you workers of lawlessness.'" Later in the same Gospel, we get the big judgment scene (Matthew 25:31–46), which sets the scene with the description "When the Son of Man comes in His glory" and concludes with the statement "These will go away into eternal punishment, but the righteous into eternal life."

Such descriptions of judgment are paralleled in Mark and Luke. In the former, for example, we read Jesus' description of the end: (Mark 13:26–27) "And then they will see the Son of Man coming in clouds with great power and glory. And then He will send out the angels and gather His elect from the four winds, from the ends of the earth to the ends of heaven." Luke includes similar passages, like this one: (Luke 21:27–28) "And then they will see the Son of Man coming in a cloud with power and great glory. Now when these things begin to take place, straighten up and raise your heads, because your redemption is drawing near."

Luke and Mark, of course, are often similar to Matthew. We even give these three Gospels a special name, *synoptic*, to mark their similarities. So it is not surprising that all three include similar descriptions of the end times and assurances regarding the Last Day from the ministry of Jesus. The Gospel of John, however, is quite different from the others in the episodes that it recounts and in the language that it uses to describe our Lord's life, work, and words. Often, the fourth evangelist seems purposefully to include episodes and themes that are not so prominent in the others and to omit others that are. The end times are one of these. They are not so prominent in John's Gospel account.

But neither are they entirely absent. In the fifth chapter of John, our Lord talked explicitly about the task of judging mankind and claimed it for His own: (v. 22) "The Father judges no one, but has given all judgment to the Son." A few verses later, the evangelist described that judgment: (vv. 28–29) "An hour is coming when all who are in the tombs will hear His voice and come out, those who have done good to the resurrection of life, and those who have done evil to the resurrection of judgment." The next chapter has similar passages, the "bread of life" discourse (such as John 6:39, 44, 54).

In John 11:24, we read that Martha, the sister of Lazarus, was relying on that promise even as she mourned her dead brother, for she told Jesus, "I know that he will rise again in the resurrection on the last day." But Jesus taught her that He was the key to that promise: (v. 25) "Whoever believes in Me, though he die, yet shall he live." So the raising of Lazarus was, in part, a demonstration that Jesus could deliver on the promise that He made regarding what was going to happen on Judgment Day regarding the resurrection of the dead.

Therefore, the "end times" are not an accidental theme in the teaching of Jesus. They are an essential part of the message He came to proclaim. Obviously, then, if we want to be faithful to that message and the Lord who gave it, we have to include His promises of reckoning and resurrection at the end of time in our own beliefs and teachings.

4 Elsewhere in the New Testament

But what about the rest of the New Testament? Do the other books discuss the last times? Indeed, yes. Although there are certainly differences in themes and emphases among the books, it is still true that besides the Gospels, the rest of the New Testament resonates with statements about the end times. In the Book of Acts, we see an affirmation of the resurrected Christ as the world's final judge in the preaching of the apostles Peter (10:42) and Paul (17:31). Paul also discussed the final judgment in his own writings; for example, Romans 2:6–8: "He [God] will render to each one according to his works: to those who by patience in well-doing seek for glory and honor and immortality, He will give eternal life; but for those who are self-seeking and do not obey the truth, but obey unrighteousness, there will be wrath and fury." Elsewhere, the apostle named Jesus as the One who is "to judge the living and the dead" (2 Timothy 4:1) and encouraged the faithful to look forward to "the appearing of the glory of our great God and Savior Jesus Christ" (Titus 2:13). Christ's second coming is an especially prominent theme in the apostle's two epistles to the Thessalonians. In the first letter, we have that powerful description of the last trumpet, at the sound of which "the dead in Christ will rise first" (4:16); and in the second letter, Paul provided an extensive discussion of when the second coming would actually occur.

Other writers besides Paul also referred to the end times. James, for example, mentioned the "coming of the Lord" (5:8), and Peter referred to the time when Christ's "glory is revealed" (1 Peter 4:13). In his second letter—as we have already seen—Peter addressed the question of why the apparent delay in Christ's return, and he affirmed confidently: (3:10) "The day of the Lord will come like a thief, and then the heavens will pass away with a roar, and the heavenly bodies will be burned up and dissolved, and the earth and the works that are done on it will be exposed."

The second coming of our Lord and a day of final judgment are prominent themes in the New Testament; and those who accept it as God's Word will recognize that such ideas were a basic part of what the first Christians taught and believed. Christianity is not just about what God has done or is still doing for people in Jesus Christ but is also about what He will do at the end of time.

5 When the End?

At the time of our Lord's ascension, the angels assured the disciples: (Acts 1:11) "This Jesus, who was taken up from you into heaven, will come again in the same way as you saw Him go into heaven." That's the promise, and the Church has confessed it ever since. But we are always tempted to ask when. When is God going to keep His Word and bring the present state of affairs to an end?

The question is a natural one, and at times of great sorrow or suffering, it may seem pressing, even urgent. However, we always have to answer that we don't know. No matter how many times we raise the question—probably as often as we hear the promise!—the answer remains the same. We don't know; nor should we. When the first Christians at Thessalonica thought that the end was imminent or, maybe, that the Lord had already come, some of them practically went to pieces. So the apostle had to write them a second time and tell them "not to be quickly shaken in mind or alarmed" (2:2). Others seem to have drawn the conclusion that there was no more point in working and carrying out their day-to-day activities, so Paul had to rebuke them: (2 Thessalonians 3:11–12) "For we hear that some among you walk in idleness, not busy at work, but busybodies. Now such persons we command and encourage in the Lord Jesus Christ to do their work quietly and to earn their own living."

So God has not told us precisely when the end will arrive. The fact of our Lord's second coming is enough. It encourages us in Christian living and sustains us in the face of suffering and evil. It is true that because Jesus is coming back, we do alter our behavior; not, however, by giving up the tasks to which God has called us, but precisely by carrying them out for the sake of others, including the great mission task that must be concluded before the end happens. "Do not grow weary in doing good" (2 Thessalonians 3:13) was Paul's advice to the Thessalonians. But that's meant for us too.

Our Lord Himself told the disciples: (Matthew 24:36) "Concerning that day and hour no one knows, not even the angels of heaven, nor the Son, but the Father only." This passage may seem unsettling at first on account of our Lord's including Himself as one who doesn't know. After all, doesn't the Bible teach that Jesus knows everything—just as Peter confessed after the resurrection (John 21:17)? Of course it does; Jesus Christ is the true God who knows and governs all things. But prior to His resurrection, Jesus "humbled" Himself by not always using His divine powers. That's why He grew hungry and thirsty, became weary when He traveled, and—as in this case—remained ignorant of when the Last Day would occur. He submitted Himself as true man to the lowliness of our situation in order that He might take our place under God's Law and save us.

So the point of Jesus' statement in Matthew 24 is to make clear that the time of His second coming is unknown to everyone and will remain unknown until it happens, for "the day of the Lord will come like a thief in the night" (1 Thessalonians 5:2).

But our ignorance of when the Last Day will arrive must not blind us to truth that it is, indeed, coming. The New Testament affirms this over and over again; and both the Gospels and Epistles include numerous "signs of the times"; that is, pointers to the coming end. For example, Jesus' last discourse in the Gospel of Matthew (ch. 24), begins with a question from the disciples, (v. 3) "What will be the sign of Your coming and of the close of the age?" The subsequent verses, therefore, contain several such indicators to remind us that the end is coming. Later in this course, we will spend some time looking at them.

In the epistles, the second chapter of 2 Thessalonians is also an important place for considering such signs, including the great end-time figure of "Antichrist." This chapter in the Bible also is a place that we will examine in this course, along with other passages that raise the issue of being ready for the end.

Also connected to the subject of signs of the end times is the Book of Revelation. This is a book of pictures and symbols, and many have gone wrong by treating at least some of the symbols as literal prophecies regarding the end. The most famous (or, rather, infamous) of these is the idea of a millennium or thousand-year reign of our Lord on earth before the Last Day. This, too, is a topic for later in the course.

But at this point, it is enough to realize that the Scriptures not only speak of the end—our Lord's second coming and a great Day of Judgment—but also urge us to be ready, in part, by recognizing the signs designated by God as reminders of what is going to happen. All things may seem to remain the same, and humanity certainly looks stuck in a rut; but the reality is far different. There is an end, and it is coming—for sure.

Conclusion

Human beings do not write their own story—however much they may think they do. Not one of us is responsible for our own beginning and, of course, we cannot avoid our own end when the time comes. But the same thing is true of all humanity. We do not write our own story. The modern world has pretty much settled on the idea that human beings—in fact, the entire universe—don't have much of a story. They are just an accident, the result of time and chance. So if the human race does come to an end, it won't much matter. In fact, it won't matter at all.

But Christians believe that a personal and loving God has written the story of mankind and that history is the record of how His story plays out in time. Like the best of stories in literature, ours, too, has a beginning, a middle, and an end. But the divine Author has prepared a conclusion far greater than any of us could write or imagine, for His story ends in glory—the glory of Jesus' return and the resurrection of God's faithful into that glory forever. And the great thing about it is this: it's not just a story.

Concluding Activities

Conclude the session with an appropriate prayer and distribute the study leaflet for week 2.

Death and Dying

Romans 6:23

Preparing for the Session

Central Focus

Participants will be reminded that besides the end of the universe, everyone has an individual end, "death," for which we must all be ready. Many people want to think of death as "natural," just a part of the way things are in a material universe. But that is not so. Death is the result of sin. Our Lord Jesus Christ has overcome sin and death so that believers can face the end of life with confidence.

Objectives

That participants, led by the Holy Spirit working through God's Word, will

1. realize that death is not a natural conclusion to human life but God's punishment for sin;
2. learn that Christ's death and resurrection are God's answer to sin and death; and
3. on account of God's love in Christ, live in expectation of eternal life and resurrection when they die.

Note for the small-group leaders: Lesson notes and other materials you will need begin on page 59.

For the Lecture Leader

Session Plan

Worship

Begin the session with the hymn printed in the study leaflet. Accompaniments are available in denominational hymnals, such as *Lutheran Service Book* or *Lutheran Worship* (refer to hymnal index). (Note: Concordia Publishing House has available *The Concordia Organist*. All the initial worship hymns in the LifeLight courses are included in this resource. It's especially helpful for mission congregations and small parishes. See the list of study resources on page 7.) Follow with this prayer:

Prayer

Heavenly Father, Lord of life, be with us as we contemplate the prospect of death and dying. Help us to realize that, just as there is forgiveness of sins in Jesus Christ, there are also resurrection and eternal life to all who believe in Him. Through the same Jesus Christ, our Lord. Amen.

Lecture Presentation

1 Introduction

Life has a rhythm that everyone must follow. Summer, fall, winter, spring. Morning then evening, then morning again, and so on. Day follows day, month follows month, year follows year. We are born, we live, we die. In a sense, therefore, we are always living in the "end times," our own personal end times, and the question of whether the universe has an end is practically irrelevant in view of our own inevitable death. And not only do human beings die, so also do the plants and animals. To be living is also to be dying. It's all quite natural.

Or is it? Since the dawn of time, human beings have worked hard to come to terms with their own dying. The death of other creatures they can well tolerate—indeed, take advantage of—but not their own. So what's going on here? Why do we die, why do we resent it, and what's to be done about it?

2 The Cycle of Life—and Death

"It won't be long now." You've heard that before. It's something we say in order to keep ourselves going when the going is rough but can't last forever. In many parts of the world, you often hear it at the end of winter. "It won't be long now." The days are getting longer and the air is getting warmer; spring will soon be here! I suppose that most of us would agree that green is better than gray and rain is better than ice, but nonetheless every season of the year brings with it its own peculiar challenges; and in many places, the coming of spring means not only putting the snow shovel away but also bringing the lawn mower out and getting ready to use it.

At those times of year when the seasons are changing, we readily recognize the cycles of nature upon which we depend and in which we participate, for just as we rejoice at the beginning of spring in the rebirth of grass and trees and flowers, we know that in just six or seven months, whatever has escaped the mower or harvester will be far along the pathway to the decay and death of winter. But what many plants experience on an annual basis is also true of human beings over a period of years. There is a cycle to life that begins with birth and ends in death: (Isaiah 40:6–7) "For all flesh is grass, and all its beauty is like the flower of the field. The grass withers, the flower fades when the breath of the LORD blows on it; surely the people are grass." Just as we can mow down the grass as soon as it grows, so time and circumstances will cut us all down and send us into the grave.

In this respect then, the only real difference between us and the plant is that we are conscious of the fate that awaits us—we recognize that death is coming. Of every newborn baby, there is always one thing that we know for sure: this baby will die. This is a horrible truth, so most of us, most of the time, try to ignore it. We also try to delay death—by diet, exercise, and medicine. And when it begins to loom over us—frightening and unavoidable—the human organism is such that we fight against death with all our might and power; but, inevitably, we lose and death wins, "for all flesh is grass."

So in this regard too, we must all admit, "It won't be long now."

But what are we supposed to do about it? Through the centuries, that has been the great question: what should we do about death? And men have proposed all kinds of answers, usually connected to some religious view or other; but for many in the modern world, increasingly the answer has become simply to accept it—accept that man is a part of nature and will die—an answer that is really no answer but is the best that modern man can come up with.

An American writer of the nineteenth century, William Cullen Bryant, expressed this point of view about as well as it could be in a poem entitled "Thanatopsis."

First of all, he describes death in unvarnished terms,

> Earth, that nourish'd thee, shall claim
> Thy growth, to be resolved to earth again,
> And, lost each human trace, surrendering up
> Thine individual being, shalt thou go
> To mix for ever with the elements,
> To be a brother to the insensible rock,
> And to the sluggish clod, which the rude swain
> Turns with his share, and treads upon.

That's it—"To mix for ever with the elements, To be a brother to the insensible rock, And to the sluggish clod"! For modern man, death is no more than a return to the impersonal nature from which humanity came forth or, as the Scriptures themselves describe it, "For you are dust and to dust you shall return" (Genesis 3:19).

But Bryant's response to death's inevitability is interesting and perhaps typical of the modern world also, for he tries to find comfort in the fact that death comes to everybody:

> As the long train
> Of ages glide away, the sons of men,
> The youth in life's green spring, and he who goes
> In the full strength of years, matron and maid,
> The speechless babe, and the gray-headed man—
> Shall one by one be gathered to thy side
> By those, who in their turn shall follow them.

Death is unavoidable, for it happens to everyone, so what's to be done? Nothing, nothing at all. Bryant urges his reader just to accept it. "Approach thy grave," he writes, "Like one who wraps the drapery of his couch About him, and lies down to pleasant dreams." End of poem, end of life.

That is very good writing, a beautiful poem, but what a desperate philosophy! However optimistically framed, Bryant's response to death undermines any form of human significance or achievement. You are a brother to the "insensible rock," or maybe a sister "to the sluggish clod"—does it really matter? Indeed, what is the point of anything—good or bad, pleasure or pain, war or peace, life or death—when "all flesh is grass, and all its beauty is like the flower of the field"?

To questions like these, "Thanatopsis" has no answer and the modern world is speechless.

3 Any Way Out?

We need to hear a voice that is louder than our own—indeed, a voice that speaks from out of a tomb, the voice of an angel, "He is not here"; the voice of a Savior, "I am the resurrection and the life"; the Word of the Lord that endures forever!

But is a word—any word—enough to counter the death that confronts us? When we see the grass withering or the corpse of a loved one entombed, how does a word—even the Word of the Scriptures—overcome that reality?

What makes the biblical Word anything more than Bryant's "Thanatopsis"?

That's a fair question, and we are right to raise it; but the answer we give is also fair and more than enough; for the Word of the Gospel is the Word of the Lord. And the Lord is the One who not only speaks but does. In fact, His speaking is His doing; so the word of resurrection is the deed of resurrection!

But before we go any further, we need to back up for a moment to realize that death—our death—is also the result of a word, God's Word, that said, "In the day that you eat of it you shall surely die" (Genesis 2:17), and that still says, "The soul who sins shall die" (Ezekiel 18:20). We do not die because it is "natural," just one of those things that happens to everybody. If that were really true, why would we fight it? Why would we care? Bryant's answer would be everyone's answer, humanity's default position in the face of death; and yet, we resist, we fight, we refuse to give in right up until our last breath, because we know—instinctively, intuitively—that death is not the way it is supposed to be. God did not make us just to die. That was not His plan, and it still isn't His plan. (Ezekiel 18:32) "For I have no pleasure in the death of anyone, declares the Lord God; so turn, and live."

Easier said than done, "Turn, and live." Adam and Eve had free will. Created without sin, they could choose the good but did not. We, however, are bound to sin and, right along with sin, to death, the punishment for sin. But we should not think that "the bondage" of our will to sin somehow excuses us from the punishment, as if really in our heart of hearts we wanted to be good but cannot. No! What we really want is to sin. Temptation comes and we give in—because we want to. That's really what is so terrible about the human condition. We want what is bad. So we deserve our punishment.

Of course, people protest this accusation. How can you say, they ask, that I want to do evil when every day I resist and refuse to do wrong? When someone angers me, don't I refrain from hitting him? Or when I would like to take something—someone else's property or maybe even someone else's spouse—don't I leave it alone? Of course you do (although not always!), but unwillingly. In your heart, you would like to give in. If you followed your desires, you would certainly succumb. So why don't you? You are afraid of scandal, or of gossip, or of getting caught. Or maybe you think that doing the "right" thing will bring a reward—a good reputation, perhaps, a chance for promotion, or maybe even that God will be pleased with your choice—but again, it's not because you really want the good in and of itself, in your heart of hearts. There—if you could only get away with it—there you want what is wrong!

The Bible teaches clearly what each of us knows about his inner self. (Genesis 8:21) "The intention of man's heart is evil from his youth." (Romans 8:7–8) "For the mind that is set on the flesh is hostile to God, for it does not submit to God's law; indeed, it cannot. Those who are in the flesh cannot please God." (Ecclesiastes 7:20) "Surely there is not a righteous man on earth who does good and never sins." Even the Christian has to admit with Paul, (Romans 7:19–20) "I do not do the good I want, but the evil I do not want is what I keep on doing. Now if I do what I do not want, it is no longer I who do it, but sin that dwells within me."

That is why we die. Not because it is "natural," but because it is punishment for our sins. And we are trapped. There's no way out. Or is there?

4 A Real Way Out

There certainly is a way out, but not because of us. One could almost say, in spite of us! (Romans 5:8) "But God shows His love for us in that while we were still sinners, Christ died for us." In this simple statement, we have the most profound truth. Our escape from death rests solely upon God's undeserved love for us in Jesus. Over and over again, the Scriptures tell us not only what God has said but also what He has done in time and space in order to rescue humanity from the curse of death by redeeming us from sin, the cause of death. God's saving activity is not a myth or pipe dream—something designed just to make us feel better in the face of the inevitable. Instead, it is reality—a reality as real as the person writing this or the person reading it or the persons hearing it read. God's Son really became a human being, really took humanity's sin upon Himself and really died on a cross to pay the penalty, and then really arose from the dead.

Many people today find the biblical accounts of our Lord's life, death, and resurrection hard to believe. But this is not just a modern phenomenon. When Paul preached about the resurrection of Jesus to the Athenian intellectuals on Mars Hill, how did they react? (Acts 17:32) "Some mocked. But others said, 'We will hear you again about this.'" They put Paul off or they scoffed at his claims. So there have always been skeptics, people like the eighteenth-century philosopher David Hume, who famously said about accounts of the miraculous, "It is contrary to experience that a miracle should be true, but not contrary to experience that testimony be false." In other words, it is more likely that the witnesses are lying or deceiving themselves than it is that a miracle has actually happened.

Maybe. Mostly. But certainly not always. God knew that people might not believe the Gospel—in fact, right from the beginning there were those who did not want to believe. Remember, for example, how the chief priests and elders reacted to the report of the guards at the tomb of Jesus (Matthew 28:11–15). What did they do? They bribed the guards to lie by saying that the disciples had stolen the body while they were sleeping! Talk about hard to believe! That unarmed and untrained disciples would take on professional soldiers to steal a corpse when they were already afraid that the authorities would be after them for their involvement with Jesus. Very unlikely, to say the least.

As strange as it may seem, however, for some—like the Jerusalem leaders—the good news is threatening. To accept the resurrection of Jesus and the rescue from death and sin that He has obtained means commitment to a new kind of life—a life no longer centered on self but on others, a life defined by faith and love. No longer self-indulgent but self-sacrificing, no longer committed to pleasure or pride or possessions, but instead to the Word and work of Christ, believers model a life that all too many resist. Believing in Jesus makes a difference—a difference that lots of people refuse. So they find (or imagine) reasons for rejecting the truth claims of the Christian religion, centering on the death and resurrection of Christ.

5 A Real Death and a Real Resurrection

Nevertheless, even in the face of such rejection, God has once again shown mercy to men and has given reasons for believing in Jesus. You can't argue someone into Christianity. It's the job of the Holy Spirit to convert. But the doubters need to deal with this, an incontrovertible truth: People just like them saw Jesus dead and then alive again.

Just recall how John began his first letter: (1 John 1:1, 3) "That which was from the beginning, which we have heard, which we have seen with our eyes, which we looked upon and have touched with our hands, concerning the word of life . . . that which we have seen and heard we proclaim also to you." John and the other disciples saw, touched, and heard the Savior as much as any of us see, touch, or hear one another. Believe it or not, therefore, there really is a way out of death. Our Lord has provided it by Himself going through it and then coming out of it on the first Easter Sunday.

Our Lord chose ordinary people like John and Simon Peter, who were fishermen, and Matthew, who was a tax collector, to witness what He was doing for mankind, because He wanted people to know about it and believe. What sort of answer to the problem of death would Jesus' resurrection be if no one had ever heard of it? So God made sure that there were witnesses.

Even the first disciples recognized the significance of such witnesses for the future of the faith, for in the days immediately after the ascension of Jesus and before Pentecost, they replaced Judas Iscariot—by that time already dead—with another man, Matthias. His qualification was that he had accompanied Jesus during His ministry (from John the Baptist to the ascension) because he was joining the apostles to become, as Peter put it, "a witness to His resurrection" (Acts 1:22). Like them, Matthias would spend the rest of his life telling others what he had seen: Jesus died but was now alive again.

By that time already, Jesus had given His Church its marching orders, with the apostles at the forefront: (Matthew 28:19) "Go therefore and make disciples of all nations." So Matthias would join the others as an official witness to the Gospel. He was a part of God's provision to publicize the saving work of Jesus, because people needed to know. Sin and death were done for, because Christ had arisen.

Later on, in his own preaching of the Gospel, Paul put the death and resurrection of Jesus at the center and presented himself as one of the divinely appointed witnesses. In fact, in his First Letter to the Corinthians, Paul listed some of those who could actually testify to the resurrection: (15:5–8) "He [Christ] appeared to Cephas, then to the twelve. Then He appeared to more than five hundred brothers at one time, most of whom are still alive, though some have fallen asleep. Then He appeared to James, then to all the apostles. Last of all, as to one untimely born, He appeared also to me." What the apostle was doing in these verses was challenging the skeptics. "If you don't believe me," he was saying, "ask the witnesses, the ordinary flesh-and-blood people who actually saw the risen Christ. And, oh, by the way, I am one of them. Years after His ascension, Jesus appeared also to me!"

So the Lord Jesus died—that's for sure; His disciples saw it. But the Lord Jesus also rose again—that's also for sure, and His disciples saw that too; indeed, they touched Him and talked with Him, for Jesus was alive! They gave their witness, even though for many of them, it cost them their lives. So hostile was the world to the Gospel that it not only ignored or scorned these first Christians but it also beat, imprisoned, and executed them. Yet they remained true to their witness because their witness was true. Jesus Christ had triumphed over death.

Therefore, this answer to death is different from all others, for it is God's answer, not man's. It is real, it is true. And because it is God's answer, this Word of the Gospel has continued to exercise power among men in all the centuries since the first Easter—power to rescue sinners by the redemption that is in the crucified and risen Lord, power to transform sin-cursed lives by the sanctifying presence of Christ's Spirit, and power to comfort and strengthen us all in the face of death.

Conclusion

Now, we began this lecture by quoting a poem that reveals the hopelessness of many in the face of inevitable death. But there's another poem that fits, and it's far better than "Thanatopsis." Written by John Donne, an Anglican clergyman, who lived a couple of centuries prior to Bryant, this poem also treats the subject of death but does so from an entirely different point of view. "Death," wrote John Donne,

> Be not proud, though some have called thee
> Mighty and dreadful, for thou are not so;
> For those whom thou think'st thou dost overthrow
> Die not, poor Death, nor yet canst thou kill me. . . .
> Why swellest thou then?
> One short sleep past, we wake eternally,
> And Death shall be no more. Death, thou shalt die!

"Death, be not proud." "Death, thou shalt die!" Those are Donne's words, but the sentiment is God's—His answer to death; God's, not man's. "Death and resurrection" are our inevitable reality because of Jesus' death and resurrection. We can count on it, because it is the promise of the Lord. "The grass withers, the flower fades, but the word of our God will stand forever" (Isaiah 40:8).

Concluding Activities

Conclude the session with an appropriate prayer and distribute the study leaflet for week 3.

Heaven or Hell

Matthew 10:28; Luke 23:46

Preparing for the Session

Central Focus

When a person dies, his soul goes to heaven or hell. All of us deserve hell on account of our sins, but Christ has opened paradise to believers.

Objectives

That participants, led by the Holy Spirit working through God's Word, will

1. understand that a person consists of body and soul;
2. learn that when a Christian dies, his soul goes to heaven; and
3. appreciate that heaven is purely a gift that God offers to sinners for the sake of Jesus.

Note for the small-group leaders: Lesson notes and other materials you will need begin on page 61.

For the Lecture Leader

Session Plan

Worship

Begin the session with the hymn printed in the study leaflet. Accompaniments are available in denominational hymnals, such as *Lutheran Service Book* or *Lutheran Worship* (refer to hymnal index). (Note: Concordia Publishing House has available *The Concordia Organist*. All the initial worship hymns in the LifeLight courses are included in this resource. It's especially helpful for mission congregations and small parishes. See the list of study resources on page 7.) Follow with this prayer:

Prayer

Dear Lord Jesus, You promised paradise to the thief on the cross and You proclaimed Your victory over sin, death, and the devil to the spirits of those in hell. Please grant that I may spend eternity with You in heaven, not hell. I confess that I do not deserve anything but punishment on account of my sins, but I trust in the forgiveness that You won for me by Your suffering and death on the cross and I hope for the eternal life that You have promised to all believers. Preserve me in the faith until my end, I pray. Amen.

Lecture Presentation

1 Introduction

"I'm but a stranger here, Heav'n is my home" (*LSB* 748). For generations, Christians have sung this hymn and others like it to express their conviction that after death, the soul of a believer lives on in heaven. It's extremely comforting to know that a loved one now dead is still with the Lord in heaven. So we repeat this thought often in the rituals that surround death and burial. But sometimes people wonder, is it true? And if it is, do we know what heaven is really like?

Over the centuries, individuals have claimed to have made contact with the dead. Even today, magazines and books publicize accounts of "near-death" experiences, the testimony of people who were thought dead but in fact came back to life. Often they tell stories of bright light, a sense of peace and security, a feeling of unconditional love, and similar phenomena. These accounts are interesting, maybe even provocative.

But we are far better off consulting the Scriptures about what happens after death. The Bible does not tell us a lot, and definitely not as much as we would like to know, but God's Word is reliable. Human stories, tales, and claims are not. Therefore, it makes a lot more sense to depend on what the Bible tells us about death and what happens next than it does to rely on whatever mankind has come up with.

2 Body and Soul

One of the first things to get straight about this topic is that every person has a soul as well as a body. Many people today are materialists. They think that the only reality is "stuff"—the stuff that our senses can perceive, whether operating on their own or with their powers enhanced by instruments like telescopes or particle accelerators. For materialists, there is no spiritual reality.

There may be unexplained phenomena like out-of-body experiences, but whatever they are, they are not the result of the spiritual intersecting the material, because the material is the only thing that exists. That means no God, no angels, and no soul.

But what does the Bible teach? (Genesis 2:7) "The Lord God formed the man of dust from the ground and breathed into his nostrils the breath of life, and the man became a living creature." Human beings consist of two principles—a material part ("dust from the ground") and an immaterial one ("the breath of life")—or what we call "body" and "soul."

Our Lord Himself taught the same truth when He gave this warning in Matthew 10:28: "Do not fear those who kill the body but cannot kill the soul. Rather fear Him who can destroy both soul and body in hell." That's pretty conclusive. Human beings are both material and immaterial—on the one hand, subject to and a part of the natural, created world; but on the other, apart from the sensible and physical, subject only to the Creator.

Some people, however, argue that man is simply an animal, a "living creature" like those mentioned in Genesis 1, when God gave orders to the waters to "swarm with swarms of living creatures" (v. 20) and to the earth to "bring forth living creatures according to their kinds—livestock and creeping things and beasts of the earth" (v. 24). After all, a living creature is a living creature, right? No, wrong! All creatures are not the same; and of none of them except human beings does the Bible say that they came alive on account of God's breath! The life principle of a human being is special and unique; we call it "the soul."

After all, Jesus Himself complained in the Garden of Gethsemane, "My soul is very sorrowful, even to death" (Matthew 26:38). His body was not yet in pain. He hadn't been whipped or beaten yet, nor was He hanging on the cross, but nevertheless, His soul was already suffering at the prospect of death, the punishment for humanity's sin. But then, with that punishment finally finished and in His last moments of dying, Jesus committed Himself to God with these words: "Father, into Your hands I commit My spirit!" (Luke 23:46). The body of Jesus was taken down from the cross, wrapped in linen, and placed into a tomb (Luke 23:53–55), but His soul went back to the Father. In His humanity, therefore, our Lord has both a body and a soul.

The events surrounding Jesus' death and resurrection demonstrate the twofold nature of human beings in still another way. Peter describes how our Lord—once more alive after His crucifixion—demonstrated His victory over death and Satan by His descent into hell: (1 Peter 3:19) "He went and proclaimed to the spirits in prison." The bodies of these unbelievers remained in the grave but their souls were in hell.

Because the Scriptures use two different words, "soul" and "spirit," when referring to humanity's immaterial principle, some theologians have thought that man has three parts: body, soul, and spirit. In all honesty, the biblical evidence is a bit ambiguous. Paul, for example, wrote in 1 Thessalonians 5:23, "Now may the God of peace Himself sanctify you completely, and may your whole spirit and soul and body be kept blameless at the coming of our Lord Jesus Christ." Obviously, the point of this prayer is that God would sanctify the entire person. But the three terms are not necessarily three parts of every individual, especially since the apostle is writing to Christians. By "spirit," he may be referring to the entire religious nature of a believer, while "soul and body" refer to the two created parts of every person. Thus, the prayer applies to what a Christian is by grace as well as by nature.

No matter how we understand 1 Thessalonians 5:23, we must not lose sight of the main point. The biblical evidence is clear: man has both a body and a soul.

3 Souls in Heaven

So what happens when a death takes place? As far as the body is concerned, the answer is obvious. Whether burned, buried, or drowned, the body undergoes a process of decay, longer or shorter, whereby its constituent elements become something other than a human body and serve other purposes in nature. As God said to Adam after he had sinned, (Genesis 3:19) "By the sweat of your face you shall eat bread, till you return to the ground, for out of it you were taken; for you are dust, and to dust you shall return."

But the fate of the body tells us nothing about the soul. Physical death is the separation of the body and the soul. We can see what happens to the body after the separation, but not the soul. So what about it? Does the soul go out of existence, unable to survive apart from the body? Does it fall asleep or otherwise become unconscious until Judgment Day? Does it take up residence in another body? Or does it continue to exist in a disembodied state somewhere and somehow outside of the physical universe until the day of resurrection?

Perhaps this last suggestion comes closest to the truth, but we have to be careful not to go beyond what the Bible says; and, in all honesty, that's not much. It is, however, more than enough to comfort Christians when they face the death of loved ones—or of themselves.

The first thing to remember is that in discussing the fate of the faithful, the primary focus of the Scriptures is on the second coming of Christ and the resurrection of the body and not on what happens to the soul at the time of temporal death. With the Corinthian Christians (1 Corinthians 1:7–8), we "wait for the revealing of our Lord Jesus Christ, who will sustain [us] to the end, guiltless in the day of our Lord Jesus Christ," and with the Philippian Christians (Philippians 3:21), we confidently hope that at His appearing, the Lord "will transform our lowly body to be like His glorious body."

But meanwhile, what happens to the soul? Where is it between death (in time) and resurrection (at the end of time)? Even phrasing the question this way is a little misleading, because time itself may not apply to the soul after death. Time is what we use to mark change in physical reality, not spiritual things. For example, we grow old (i.e., our bodies change in size, abilities, and health), but does age apply to the soul? This seems doubtful; but even if it were true, an "old" soul would be far different from an "old" body. So maybe time does not apply to souls in heaven, and they are not just "waiting around" for the Last Day. Maybe temporal death takes the soul instantaneously to Judgment Day and resurrection—but then again, maybe not. We have to be very careful that we do not turn our speculations into fact.

Probably a good place to start answering the question of what about the soul is with the death of Jesus. As He breathed His last, He confidently called out, "Father, into Your hands I commit My spirit!" (Luke 23:46). Having completed the work for which the Father had sent Him, Jesus died, knowing that His soul would remain secure in the hands of God.

It made all the sense in the world for Jesus to commend His soul to God, but what about us? We may think that such confident commitment can hardly be fitting for sinners like us. But it is, because God is our Father too. This is one of the grand themes of Jesus' ministry, evident, for example, in the Lord's Prayer: "Our Father who art in heaven . . ." Paul clearly taught this as well: (Galatians 4:4–6) "God sent forth His Son . . . to redeem those who were under the law, so that we might receive adoption as sons. And because you are sons, God has sent the Spirit of His Son into our hearts, crying, 'Abba! Father!'"

Apart from Christ, we are still in our sins and so at enmity with God (Romans 8:7). Judgment awaits us at the moment of death (Hebrews 9:27). But by Baptism, we are clothed with Christ (Galatians 3:27), and in faith, we are sons and heirs right along with Christ (Galatians 4:7). Like Jesus, therefore, we too can call upon God confidently as our Father right at the time we are breathing our last, "Father, into Your hands I commit my spirit."

So we start with the general principle—a promise actually—that when a Christian dies, his body stays here to await the resurrection and his soul goes back to God. This is what the Preacher wrote in Ecclesiastes 12:7: "The dust returns to the earth as it was, and the spirit returns to God who gave it." There is more to say, of course, but no real need to say it. The hands of our heavenly Father are good ones, so the souls of the faithful are just fine when God reaches out to receive them at the time of death.

There are a couple of other passages in which the Bible hints at just how well off the believers' souls are after death. In his Letter to the Philippians, Paul shared with his readers some thoughts about the future. He was in prison. On the one hand, the authorities could release him and his work as an apostle would continue. That would be good for the Church. On the other hand, Paul's imprisonment might end in his death. So how did he feel about that? He wrote: (Philippians 1:21, 23) "For to me to live is Christ, and to die is gain. . . . I am hard pressed between the two. My desire is to depart and be with Christ, for that is far better." Note well: Death for the Christian is better than earthly life!

But how far is "far better"? Again, we do not know, and it's virtually impossible to describe something "immaterial" like the soul without using material images. Nevertheless, the apostle knew that death was not the end, nor merely a holding pattern for the soul until Judgment Day, but a continued personal existence with the Savior, and that had to be not just good but the best!

There's still another passage that suggests the degree of goodness to which we may look forward at the time of death. This is the Word of Jesus to the thief on the cross who asked our Lord to remember him when He came into His kingdom. At once, Jesus responded with a promise: (Luke 23:43) "Truly, I say to you, today you will be with Me in Paradise." Wow! Paradise! It doesn't get any better than that. This is the word in the Greek

Old Testament that is applied to the Garden of Eden (such as in Genesis 2:8, 10). It is also used in Revelation 2:7 in connection with a reward for faithfulness and in 2 Corinthians 12:3 as a place to which God transported the apostle, the "third heaven" (v. 2).

But can we say anything about life in this paradise of heaven other than that it is very, very good? Again, without going into details about the nature of an immaterial existence (life without a body), we are certainly safe in saying what won't be there: sin and its consequences. This is one of the reasons that Scripture refers to life in heaven as "rest." All of the things that grieve and afflict us will be gone. Therefore, in the Book of Revelation (14:13), John heard a voice from heaven that said, "'Write this: Blessed are the dead who die in the Lord from now on.' 'Blessed indeed,' says the Spirit, 'that they may rest from their labors.'" "Blessed" is not a word that fits life here. We are blessed, of course. But earthly existence is filled with challenges and difficulties, some of our own making and others not. Being alive means, at best, experiencing the bad with the good. But "blessed" does describe heaven. There, the battles of life—physical and spiritual—are done with. Life goes on, a personal relationship with God goes on, but the souls of the faithful no longer experience wickedness and evil, pain and suffering, sorrow and death. Those are gone forever.

The first Christian martyr, Stephen, got a glimpse into heaven at the time of his death. By the power of the Holy Spirit, he "gazed into heaven and saw the glory of God, and Jesus standing at the right hand of God." What a wonderful blessing! Just moments before his enemies began to rain down rocks upon his head and crush his body, Stephen was strengthened by God for his end by this vision of Christ in heaven. In faith, therefore, Stephen died like his Lord—with a prayer for his foes and by entrusting himself to the Savior Himself: "Lord Jesus, receive my spirit" (Acts 7:55).

There are several aspects to Stephen's death that are unique to him. After all, he was the first to face death for the sake of Christ after Pentecost. But he also exemplifies what is true for every Christian. At the time of physical death, a believer continues to live in and with the Lord. Jesus Himself has promised: (John 11:25–26) "I am the resurrection and the life. . . . Everyone who lives and believes in Me shall never die." God never speaks idly. He means what He says, and we can trust it. We may not understand how it all works out, but we know who is making the promise—and that is all that we really need to know.

4 Mercy and Faith

But to whom is God making this promise? Who is really going to heaven when they die? After all, there are very few Stephens among us. He met his end not from accident, disease, or old age but because of his witnessing to Jesus, his speaking up for the Lord when some powerful folks didn't want to hear it. So maybe he deserved to go to heaven when he died. But what about it? Who actually makes it in?

Well, nobody deserves heaven—not even Stephen. And remember, Jesus first gave the promise of paradise not to some great saint—a confessor, a martyr, someone self-giving to the end—but to a criminal on a cross (Luke 23:39–43). It's true, of course, that in the last moments of his life, this man recognized who Jesus was and went so far as to tell his fellow criminal to be quiet when he was making fun of the Lord. But did that make up for the crimes that had brought him to the cross? Hardly. He went to paradise solely because of God's mercy.

And that's how it is for everybody. God's mercy toward sinners is the key to heaven. It doesn't take long for everyone to realize that we all fail to measure up to what God expects from people, as expressed, for example, in the Ten Commandments. For sure, we may never have committed murder, but Jesus explained: (Matthew 5:22) "Everyone who is angry with his brother will be liable to judgment. . . . Whoever says, 'You fool!' will be liable to the hell of fire." Likewise, with respect to the rest of the Commandments, sin is present in the heart even if it never results in outward actions. And none of us—not even the best—actually avoids the outward actions that reveal the sin in our hearts, at least not all the time.

The Bible says: (Romans 3:23) "All have sinned and fall short of the glory of God." Of course, since it's in the Bible, we'd better believe it, but it's not just "in the Bible." We know it's true from experience also. We can certainly see sin in others (and we love to talk about it!), but basic honesty should lead each of us to see it in ourselves as well and to admit it. After all, Jesus would not instruct us to pray "and forgive us our trespasses" if He knew we were never going to sin.

In fact, the only one who did not sin and so deserved to go to heaven was none other than our Lord Himself. It is precisely on His account that heaven is open to us: (John 3:16) "For God so loved the world, that He gave His only Son, that whoever believes in Him should not perish but have eternal life."

God's mercy opens up heaven to us, and through faith in the Savior, we walk right in. That is the Gospel. Christ our Savior did the work. He kept the Law, He paid the price, and He offers it all to us in His Word. We simply need to receive it, trusting the promise, and it's all ours. And the Holy Spirit even does that for us. He converts us from unbelief to belief, so faith is God's gift too—right along with forgiveness now and heaven when we die.

5 Hell

So what about those who refuse to believe? Is heaven open for them? It's open, yes, but they're not going to enter. This brings us to the doctrine of hell. Popular culture has a fascination with everlasting punishment, as illustrated by popular songs such as "Lake of Fire" released by the Meat Puppets in 1984, and famously performed by Kurt Cobain in 1993, a former Christian who took his own life a year later.

Christians may not like to discuss hell. We may not even like to think about it. A place of eternal suffering? It's painful even to imagine it. So we don't do so unless forced to. But the doctrine of the last things does precisely that. We have to talk about hell while making absolutely certain that the promise of heaven gets through, praying that it inspires comfort and hope for those who hear us.

First of all, hell exists. The Scriptures teach this clearly in, for example, 1 Peter 3:19–20. Our Lord, "put to death in the flesh but made alive in the spirit, . . . went and proclaimed to the spirits in prison, because they formerly did not obey, when God's patience waited in the days of Noah." Here, hell is called "prison" and is described as a destination for "spirits" who did not "obey."

As with heaven, it is difficult to describe a "spiritual" existence without using "material" images. But clearly, hell is a place of suffering that no one would want to experience. Jesus described it (Matthew 8:12) as a place of "outer darkness. . . . There will be weeping and gnashing of teeth." Elsewhere, He spoke of "the hell of fire" (Matthew 5:22); and in the parable of the rich man and Lazarus, he described the former as ending up "in torment" and asking Abraham for just a drop of water to cool his tongue for, as he said, "I am in anguish in this flame" (Luke 16:23–24).

Clearly, no one wants to spend eternity in a place that the Scriptures identify with the pain of burning, and no one has to. We deserve hell on account of our sinfulness, but we don't have to go there. Jesus said, (John 3:17) "God did not send His Son into the world to condemn the world, but in order that the world might be saved through Him." Nevertheless, He added, (v. 18) "Whoever does not believe is condemned already, because he has not believed in the name of the only Son of God." God gives us a way out, but we need to take it—by faith.

Conclusion

So which will it be? Heaven or hell? These are real places and the only two destinations for the soul at the time of death. Christians, take comfort in the promises and teachings of God about your final destination! God did not make us for death and damnation, and even when man sinned, God did not let His anger pronounce the last word. He promised a Savior who would crush the serpent's head (Genesis 3:15). Jesus endured death so that we may have life; Jesus now is seated at the Father's right hand, interceding for you.

As often as you mention hell to others, be sure you follow through and discuss heaven. Point them on high, emphasize the Lord's promises, and fill their ears with the message of His love of God for all and for them. The Savior has come and opened the doorway to heaven. Through the Gospel Word of forgiveness, heaven is ours both at the moment of death and for all eternity. Thank God for His mercy in Jesus!

Concluding Activities

Conclude the session with an appropriate prayer and distribute the study leaflet for week 4.

Judgment in the Old Testament

Psalm 96:12–13

Preparing for the Session

Central Focus

We can see that from the first days of human history, God has punished wickedness. This is a theme that permeates the Old Testament, but judgment is also associated with the coming of the Messiah. That same figure is portrayed as the Redeemer through whom God will show mercy to the penitent.

Objectives

That participants, led by the Holy Spirit working through God's Word, will

1. realize that God's punishment of the wicked is a principal theme of the Old Testament;
2. understand that God also offers mercy and forgiveness in the Old Testament; and
3. learn that God's Word will prepare them for the judgment that will culminate in the coming of the Messiah.

Note for the small-group leaders: Lesson notes and other materials you will need begin on page 64.

For the Lecture Leader

Session Plan

Worship

Begin the session with the hymn printed in the study leaflet. Accompaniments are available in denominational hymnals, such as *Lutheran Service Book* or *Lutheran Worship* (refer to hymnal index). (Note: Concordia Publishing House has available *The Concordia Organist.* All the initial worship hymns in the LifeLight courses are included in this resource. It's especially helpful for mission congregations and small parishes. See the list of study resources on page 7.) Follow with this prayer:

Prayer

Heavenly Father, You destroyed the world of Noah's day with a flood, and the cities of Sodom and Gomorrah with fire from heaven, to show that You punish sin and sinners who refuse to repent. Please move me always to confess my sins plainly and truthfully to You and to put all my hope in Your promises of forgiveness that You have made to me and all people for the sake of Jesus, my Lord and Savior. In His name I pray. Amen.

Lecture Presentation

1 Introduction

Will God finally act to set things right? Throughout the ages—and we still hear it today—many Christians have asked this question in the face of (apparently) triumphant evil. In our times, it arises especially on account of the collapse of Christian culture. A couple of generations ago, the customs and mores of society, though never perfect, seemed to reinforce biblical values. But today that's all different. The legalization of abortion and the normalization of sodomy are two issues that immediately come to mind that illustrate this point. So we ask whether God is ever going to do something about it. When will He follow through and enforce the moral principles He has set into the world, let alone revealed in the Scriptures?

Of course, we don't know when—and efforts to figure it out are really misguided. But we do know that a time of judgment is coming. Not only does our Lord Jesus Christ tell us and predict it, many "preliminary" judgments have already taken place. Even though we associate "Judgment Day" with the New Testament, in which our Lord and His apostles promise, describe, and provide signs of its coming, the idea of judgment is already pervasive in the Old Testament.

Will He really come to "judge the living and the dead"? We have every confidence that He certainly will, simply on the basis of what God has said and done before Jesus came the first time!

2 God's Judgment over All People

The Old Testament is filled with talk about judgment, and not just talk. Major episodes of biblical history demonstrate this truth as well. Words and deeds both make "judgment" one of the great themes in the first part of the Bible. Psalm 96, for example, points forward to Judgment Day by concluding with these lines: (vv. 12–13) "Then shall all the trees of the forest sing for joy before the Lord, for He comes, for He comes to judge the earth. He will judge the world in righteousness, and the peoples in His faithfulness." Similar references abound, too numerous, really, to list. The entire Book of Joel is a vision of judgment, "the day of the Lord"; and, of course, many of the prophets pronounce judgment upon fallen Israel.

Psalm 50 is a powerful presentation of this Old Testament theme, God's judgment of Israel. In verses 1–6, the poet describes the coming of the Lord to judge. He summons the entire world into His presence—a presence that is accompanied by a "devouring fire" and a "mighty tempest," signs in nature that are reminiscent of the giving of the Law on Mount Sinai (such as in Exodus 19:18–20; 20:18–19). He focuses His judgment upon His "faithful ones," that is, the people of Israel who made a "covenant" with Him. Then He presents, first of all, His indictment (Psalm 50:7–15). What is it that the people have done wrong? He does not accuse them of having failed in their outer duties, their sacrifices. No, they had performed them regularly, but God certainly doesn't need such things. After all, He rules and possesses all the animals of the world. So their sacrifices were insufficient, because the people failed to recognize God really as their God, from whom all blessings came and to whom they owed their vows, their prayers, and their thanksgivings. Without such commitment in their hearts, their sacrifices were pointless.

Thus, the faithful stand under judgment, but so do the wicked (vv. 16–21). In His accusations against them, God singles out their hypocritical worship, their admiration for thieves and adulterers, their lies and their slander. They think they have gotten away with all of this because they think God is like them in their tolerance of evil. But not so. God concludes His admonition (vv. 22–23) with a threat ("lest I tear you apart") and a promise ("I will show the salvation of God").

But not only Israel stands under the judgment of God. The Old Testament also speaks about God's judgment against others. Several of the prophets pronounce doom against Israel's neighbors and enemies. Isaiah prophesies judgment against the nations in chapters 13–23; Jeremiah does so in chapters 46–51; Ezekiel in chapters 25–32; Amos in chapters 1 and 2; and Zephaniah in chapters 2 and 3. Obadiah's message is almost completely a condemnation of Edom, and Nahum's of Nineveh. So God's judgment is universal. It covers all humanity.

But isn't this what we should expect? After all, at the beginning, when humanity did not yet consist of Jews and Gentiles but of just two people—two people who disobeyed their Maker—what happened? Well, in Genesis 3, the sin of Adam and Eve resulted in a curse upon all women (v. 16) and all men (vv. 17–19); and in Romans 5:12, Paul reminds us, "Therefore, just as sin came into the world through one man [Adam], and death through sin, and so death spread to all men because all sinned." Universal sin brings universal punishment. God's judgment plays no favorites; He applies it to all.

3 Not Just Talk

In the Old Testament, we not only read about pronouncements of judgment but we also see how God carries out His threats. One of the best-known of God's punishments was His destruction of Sodom and Gomorrah, described in Genesis 19:24–25: "Then the Lord rained on Sodom and Gomorrah sulfur and fire from the Lord out of heaven. And He overthrew those cities, and all the valley, and all the inhabitants of the cities, and what grew on the ground." God had heard the "outcry" (Genesis 18:20; 19:13) against the wickedness of those cities—a wickedness confirmed by their despicable intentions directed toward the angelic visitors (Genesis 19:4–5). So God proceeded with the punishment. It was total and final.

But the people of Sodom and Gomorrah were contemporaries of Abraham, not his descendants. Nevertheless, on account of their sins too, God carried out judgment against the children of Israel. The division of Israel into two separate kingdoms following the death of Solomon was itself a judgment upon the late king because he had turned away from the Lord to worship false gods (1 Kings 11:9–13). But then when each part of the divided kingdom persisted in sins of apostasy and idolatry, God's judgment fell upon them.

In 2 Kings 17:6, for example, we read about the end of the Northern Kingdom of Israel: "The king of Assyria captured Samaria [the capital of Israel] and he carried the Israelites away to Assyria." But why did this happen? Predicted already in the days of the Northern Kingdom's first king, Jeroboam (1 Kings 14:15), Israel's destruction was God's final judgment upon Israel's sins: (2 Kings 17:7–12) "And this occurred because the people of Israel had sinned against the Lord their God . . . and had feared other gods . . . and they served idols, of which the Lord had said to them, 'You shall not do this.'"

And how about the Babylonian Captivity? This calamity fell upon the Southern Kingdom of Judah more than a century after the destruction of the north. Once again, on account of Judah's sins, God had threatened: (2 Kings 23:27) "I will remove Judah also out of My sight, as I have removed Israel, and I will cast off this city that I have chosen, Jerusalem, and the house [i.e., the temple] of which I said, My name shall be there." And what happened? God followed through on His threat. So in 2 Kings 25, we read about Nebuchadnezzar's siege of Jerusalem (v. 1) and the destruction of the temple (v. 9) and then, finally, "Judah was taken into exile out of its land" (v. 21). God is not mocked. He demands obedience from His people, and when it is not forthcoming, judgment follows.

By far the best-known of God's judgments in the Old Testament is the flood—a direct precursor of the final Judgment Day: (Matthew 24:37, 39) "For as were the days of Noah, so will be the coming of the Son of Man. . . . They were unaware until the flood came and swept them all away, so will be the coming of the Son of Man." The destruction caused by the flood was horrific, almost unimaginable: (Genesis 7:21–23) "And all flesh died that moved on the earth, birds, livestock, beasts, all swarming creatures that swarm on the earth, and all mankind. Everything on the dry land in whose nostrils was the breath of life died. He blotted out every living thing that was on the face of the ground, man and animals and creeping things and birds of the heavens. They were blotted out from the earth."

The destruction was virtually total and included birds, reptiles, and animals as well as people. But why? Why this horror? God leaves us in no doubt at all about why He sent the flood: (Genesis 6:5–7) "The Lord saw that the wickedness of man was great in the earth, and that every intention of the thoughts of his heart was only evil continually. And the Lord was very sorry that He had made man on the earth, and it grieved Him to His heart. So the Lord said, 'I will blot out man whom I have created from the face of the land, man and animals and creeping things and birds of the heavens, for I am sorry that I have made them.'"

God punishes sin. It's that simple. He does not ignore it or let it slide. He is not ignorant of what is going on, and He is not indifferent to what He sees. Wickedness angers Him. He will punish it. He has sent judgment before, and He will do so again. The entire Old Testament is clear about that.

4 And Not Just Punishment!

But that is not the complete story, is it? For while God was destroying the world and its inhabitants in the great flood, He was also preserving Noah, his family, and animals in the ark (Genesis 7:1–5). And when He sent fire and brimstone upon Sodom and Gomorrah, He also rescued Lot and his daughters (Genesis 19:29). And even though He sent Judah into exile, He also restored His people to the Promised Land when the time of their captivity was over (2 Chronicles 36:22–23).

So although the Old Testament is certainly clear about the righteous anger of God, directed against the sinfulness of man, there is a prominent subtheme in the first part of the Scriptures as well—that God is patient, merciful, and forgiving. Just think about how God operated through the centuries of Israel's history—from the days of the exodus all the way through the return from captivity. At every step of the way, when the children of Israel succumbed to temptation, God sent warnings, then punishment, then restoration. Isn't this the pattern, for example, in the Book of Judges? The second chapter explains how it went during this period of Israel's history: (v. 11) "And the people of Israel did what was evil in the sight of the Lord and served the Baals"; (v. 14) "so the anger of the Lord was kindled against Israel, and He gave them over to plunderers, who plundered them. And He sold them into the hand of their surrounding enemies, so that they could no longer withstand their enemies"; and (v. 18) "whenever the Lord raised up judges for them, the Lord was with the judge, and he saved them from the hand of their enemies all the days of the judge. For the Lord was moved to pity by their groaning because of those who afflicted and oppressed them." God punished the people for their sins but "was moved to pity" by their groanings under punishment and so sent deliverance through the judges.

Later, when God sent prophets, much of their message was condemnation, to be sure, but not exclusively. They also pointed to God's grace and promised hope. For example, even though a theme of judgment against sin dominates the first part of Isaiah (chs. 1–39), God's grace prevails to such a degree in the second part of the book (chs. 40–66) that the prophet has been called, "the Fifth Evangelist"! Even the "weeping prophet," Jeremiah, who throughout his book castigates the people for their idolatry in the fiercest language, nevertheless comforts them with the promise of a new relationship with God based on the forgiveness of sins (Jeremiah 31:31–34).

One of the more interesting demonstrations of God's mercy in the prophets occurred in connection with Jonah's ministry to the pagan city of Nineveh, capital of the fierce and dreaded Assyrians. It is no wonder that Jonah first fled when the Lord ordered him, (Jonah 1:2) "Arise, go to Nineveh . . . and call out against it, for their evil has come up before Me"; but after failing to escape, Jonah did what was required and entered Nineveh with a message of doom: (3:4) "Yet forty days, and Nineveh shall be overthrown." But soon thereafter, Jonah became angry with God, because He did not follow through on His threat. Instead, when the king of Nineveh led his people in repentance, the Lord relented and did not send the disaster Jonah had predicted. As Jonah said, (4:2) "I knew that You are a gracious God and merciful, slow to anger and abounding in steadfast love, and relenting from disaster." So even in the case of pure pagans, God's condemnation was not His last word. Instead, His last word was mercy!

This should not be a surprise, for we see it already in the first days of human history. Now, if there was anybody who ever deserved God's wrath and destruction, it has to be Adam and Eve. Their existence was blessed beyond imagining, their obligation to refrain from eating the fruit of but one tree was practically trivial, and yet they gave in to a temptation that was foolish on its face: "You will be like God" (Genesis 3:5) indeed! They already were like God, created in His image (1:27), so what more could they want?

So God did punish them. He cursed the ground (Genesis 3:17–18); He burdened childbirth (v. 16); He pronounced a sentence of death (v. 19). And, oh, yes, He condemned the serpent that had functioned as Satan's mouthpiece (v. 14). But just as God was addressing the devilish snake, He included a word of promise, a ray of hope, a prospect of redemption: (3:15) "I will put enmity between you and the woman, and between your offspring and her offspring; He shall bruise your head, and you shall bruise His heel."

How amazing! How extraordinary! God's condemnation is not His last word to humanity, for He also promises the offspring of a woman to crush the serpent's head. In some ways, this first Gospel Word raises more questions than it answers about how God would actually work out man's salvation. We can imagine Adam and Eve discussing together what it meant and wondering how God was going to accomplish His Word. Luther thought that Eve expected her son Cain already to be the Savior! Only with additional promises like those to Abraham and to David, and with prophecies like those of Isaiah, did the first Gospel Word become clearer. And finally, with its fulfillment in Jesus, it became clear once and for all. But it was there from the beginning to create and nurture faith. In the face of God's just judgment against sin, there was still hope in His promise of deliverance and of a Deliverer!

5 The Messiah as Judge

Other Old Testament passages elaborate on the messianic hope first articulated in Genesis 3:15; but in connection with judgment specifically, one of the most significant is Isaiah 11:1–9. The prophet begins (v. 1) by describing the Coming One as "a shoot from the stump of Jesse," David's father. Thus, He will be a new David but coming out of the same family, now reduced, however, to just a "stump" (think of the humble condition of Mary and Joseph). But the Spirit of the Lord is upon Him (v. 2), and so He exercises perfect judgment (vv. 3–4). Justice, of course, is the task of any king, but how many earthly rulers actually act justly? But the One prophesied here certainly will: (v. 4) "With righteousness He shall judge the poor, and decide with equity for the meek of the earth; and He shall strike the earth with the rod of His mouth, and with the breath of His lips He shall kill the wicked." Unlike the unjust rulers described earlier in the book, this new David acts on behalf of the downtrodden and punishes evildoers. Subsequent to His exercising judgment, a new kingdom arises, described in idyllic terms by the prophet: (vv. 6–9) "The wolf shall dwell with the lamb" and so on—pictures of peace that point forward to a new world, one that follows and does away with an old world of sin and wickedness. The new king brings forward a new world.

Another messianic passage in the Old Testament that is even more directly related to Judgment Day as described in the New is Daniel 7:13–14: "I [Daniel] saw in the night visions, and behold, with the clouds of heaven there came one like a son of man. . . . And to Him was given dominion and glory and a kingdom, that all peoples, nations, and languages should serve Him; His dominion is an everlasting dominion, which shall not pass away, and His kingdom one that shall not be destroyed."

This particular passage belongs to those chapters in Daniel that remind us of the Book of Revelation, populated as they are with strange and symbolic creatures; for instance, the beast with ten horns (Daniel 7:19–20). In fact, in a couple of places, Revelation uses language that is very similar to Daniel's; such as (Revelation 14:14) "Then I looked, and behold, a white cloud, and seated on the cloud one like a son of man, with a golden crown on His head, and a sharp sickle in His hand." But for our purposes, the passage in Daniel is noteworthy especially because our Lord applied it to His own second coming. When asked by the Sanhedrin at the time of His trial whether He was the Messiah, the Son of God, Jesus answered: (Mark 14:62) "I am, and you will see the Son of Man seated at the right hand of Power, and coming with the clouds of heaven." Even before that climactic moment, our Lord had employed the same language in His description of the Last Day: (Luke 21:27) "And then they will see the Son of Man coming in a cloud with power and great glory."

What this demonstrates, therefore, is that Judgment Day—a final reckoning over mankind by the Messiah—was a part of Old Testament revelation long before the Messiah actually arrived to inaugurate the era of the New Testament.

Conclusion

The New Testament clearly teaches a second coming of Christ. But this is a fulfillment of what the Old Testament already taught. The picture of God in the Old Testament presents us with two great truths: God's justice (He punishes sin) and His mercy (He also forgives it). This double truth was clear right from the beginning after Adam and Eve's sin, and it runs through the rest of the Scriptures. But how do we reconcile justice with mercy? They don't seem a very comfortable fit. Either God punishes or He forgives. He cannot do both—or can He?

In the Messiah, these two truths come together. Since He is the Suffering Servant of Isaiah 53, the Savior offers Himself as our substitute to pay for our sins. Justice and mercy come together in Him. But in Isaiah 11 and Daniel 7, we also see Him as the world's final Judge and King. He provides a final reckoning for those who reject His offer of grace in order to persist in their wickedness.

Just as God's faithful people prior to the first coming of Christ had to await His arrival for centuries, so today we are waiting for His second coming to set everything right again. This will certainly happen. The fruits of His victory on the cross and at the tomb will find their fulfillment in a final judgment that destroys wickedness and makes all things new again.

Concluding Activities

Conclude the session with an appropriate prayer and distribute the study leaflet for week 5.

Judgment Day

Matthew 25:31–46

Preparing for the Session

Central Focus

Judgment Day is an essential aspect of the work of Jesus. John the Baptist prophesied it, and Jesus Himself promised it and described it. In order to be ready for Judgment Day, the basic requirement is faith. But true faith is always active in love toward one's neighbor. That will be evident to all on the Last Day.

Objectives

That participants, led by the Holy Spirit working through God's Word, will

1. realize that judging the living and dead at the end of time is an essential aspect of the work of Jesus;
2. understand that the only real preparation for Judgment Day is repentance and faith; and
3. exercise true faith active in love.

Note for the small-group leaders: Lesson notes and other materials you will need begin on page 67.

For the Lecture Leader

Session Plan

Worship

Begin the session with the hymn printed in the study leaflet. Accompaniments are available in denominational hymnals, such as *Lutheran Service Book* or *Lutheran Worship* (refer to hymnal index). (Note: Concordia Publishing House has available *The Concordia Organist.* All the initial worship hymns in the LifeLight courses are included in this resource. It's especially helpful for mission congregations and small parishes. See the list of study resources on page 7.) Follow with this prayer:

Prayer

Heavenly Father, who is righteous and holy but also all-merciful, enable us to stand in the Day of Judgment through repentance and faith. Renew our lives through Your Holy Spirit so that, truly believing in Christ our Savior, we may serve You by serving others in accordance with Your Word. Through the same Jesus Christ, our Savior. Amen.

Lecture Presentation

1 Introduction

Judgment Day! A time of final reckoning, of making everything right again, and of getting what you deserve. Used these days in films, books, and everyday speech, we may forget that the origin of "Judgment Day" is biblical. The Bible teaches that the world will end when our Lord returns "to judge the living and the dead." That will be the ultimate reckoning, the Last Day, the end.

Literary, movie, and conversational references to Judgment Day we can safely ignore, but not what the Bible says. God's Word determines what is and what will happen. Just think of creation: God spoke and it was done. Just think of salvation: God promised a Savior and He came. So too with the end. God has told us a great deal about a final judgment—and what He has said will take place. You can count on it.

2 John the Baptist

The New Testament era begins with John the Baptist—or is he really the end of the Old? One can make an argument for either. On the one hand, John is definitely the forerunner of Jesus and presents the same basic message as our Lord: "Repent, for the kingdom of heaven is at hand" (Matthew 3:2—John; Matthew 4:17—Jesus). This seems to make John a part of the new era; but other passages place him in the old. Our Lord Himself said of John: (Matthew 11:11) "Among those born of women there has arisen no one greater than John the Baptist. Yet the one who is least in the kingdom of heaven is greater than he." How can this be? Clearly, our Lord is not challenging either the faith or ministry of John the Baptist. But nonetheless it is true that we who are believers today—on this side of the cross and empty tomb—have a much greater understanding of how God keeps His promises. In other words, we are greater because of God's greater gifts, namely, His revelation in the New Testament. The Baptist was dead before Christ had completed His saving work.

From this perspective, therefore, John's presentation of Jesus has more in common with the prophets of the Old Testament than with apostles and evangelists of the New. John's preaching picks up where Malachi's had left off. In fact, John is the fulfillment of Malachi's prediction that Elijah would come again (Malachi 4:5), as our Lord Himself pointed out, "He is Elijah who is to come" (Matthew 11:14).

But Malachi is also one of the prophets of judgment in the Old Testament who reminded his hearers of a Great Day of the Lord: (Malachi 4:1–2) "For behold, the day is coming, burning like an oven, when all the arrogant and all evildoers will be stubble. The day that is coming shall set them ablaze, says the Lord of hosts, so that it will leave them neither root nor branch. But for you who fear My name, the sun of righteousness shall rise with healing in its wings." For Malachi, then, the work of the Messiah would be one of judgment, intended to rescue the faithful from the wicked and to vindicate them: (4:3) "You shall tread down the wicked, for they will be ashes under the soles of your feet, on the day when I act, says the Lord of hosts."

So judgment is on its way, "a great and awesome day of the Lord." And to prepare the people for that day, God also promised a forerunner, whose work Malachi summarized in the very last verse of his book: (4:6) "And he will turn the hearts of fathers to their children and the hearts of children to their fathers, lest I come and strike the land with a decree of utter destruction." The angel Gabriel used these words in describing John to his father, Zechariah (Luke 1:16–17). So John was to be a reconciler of fathers and children, and he did so by preaching a message of repentance.

But for our purposes, the main point is that in the immediate background to John's understanding of the work of the Messiah was the prospect of Judgment Day. John was supposed to get the people ready for that. And he did.

As noted before, Matthew summarized the preaching of John with the statement "Repent, for the kingdom of heaven is at hand" (Matthew 3:1). But what did John mean? "Repent" is practically self-explanatory. John wanted the people to recognize their sins. He baptized them for the "forgiveness of sins," and as he did so, they confessed their sins (Mark 1:4–5). But to repent also meant a change of life, since John urged his hearers to "bear fruits in keeping with repentance" (Luke 3:8) and provided specific examples for tax collectors and soldiers as well as exhortations in general about sharing one's clothing and food with those who have none (Luke 3:10–14). So repentance included both recognition and reform, acknowledging one's sin and changing one's life.

But why? Why should people "repent"? John said, "For the kingdom of heaven is at hand" (Matthew 3:2). That term, "kingdom of heaven" (or "of God"), is an important one in the Scriptures. It occurs over eighty times in the first three Gospels (thirty-seven in Matthew; fourteen in Mark; and thirty-two in Luke) and covers a wide range of meanings. But in certain contexts, it points decisively to Judgment Day. For example, Jesus spoke of blessing and judgment in Matthew 8:11–12: "Many will come from east and west and recline at table with Abraham, Isaac, and Jacob in the kingdom of heaven, while the sons of the kingdom will be thrown into the outer darkness." Here, Jesus must have shocked His hearers by including Gentiles with the patriarchs in the future blessings of the Kingdom but excluding the chosen people when judgment occurs.

In the preaching of John the Baptist, the theme of judgment is prominent; for instance, (Matthew 3:10) "Every tree therefore that does not bear good fruit is cut down and thrown into the fire" and (v. 12) "His winnowing fork is in His hand, and He will clear His threshing floor and gather His wheat into the barn, but the chaff he will burn with unquenchable fire." Luke recorded a similar description of the preaching of John—judgment is surely coming, so now is the time to repent (Luke 3:7–17).

3 Jesus the Judge

So John picked up where the Old Testament left off in pointing the people forward to the judgment of God; but he also made it clear that God would exercise this judgment through the Coming One. "He who is coming after me," he said, "is mightier than I" and He would be the one to gather the wheat and burn the chaff (Matthew 3:11–12). Shortly thereafter, Jesus came forward for Baptism by John, and God the Father and the Spirit designated Him as the one to fulfill John's prediction, so that John could say: (John 1:34) "I have seen and have borne witness that this [namely, Jesus] is the Son of God."

This witness of John the Baptist—that Jesus is the promised Messiah—was picked up by the rest of the New

Testament. Over and over again, the Old Testament was cited to prove that Jesus fulfilled what the Old Testament prophesied. Matthew, for example, included four such references in the first two chapters of his Gospel account, "All this took place to fulfill what the Lord had spoken by the prophet" (Matthew 1:22); and toward the end of his Gospel, John likewise pointed out that the soldiers did not break Jesus' legs "that the Scripture might be fulfilled" (John 19:36). Our Lord Himself claimed, (Luke 24:44) "Everything written about Me in the Law of Moses and the Prophets and the Psalms must be fulfilled," and He asserted to His enemies, (John 5:39) "You search the Scriptures because you think that in them you have eternal life; and it is they that bear witness about Me."

But as we have seen in the previous lecture, a part of what the Old Testament taught about judgment was that God would carry it out through the Messiah. So this is what John the Baptist taught too. "Repent, for the Lord is coming as Judge" is one way of paraphrasing his message. Perhaps this is one of the reasons why John later—after his imprisonment by Herod—sent his disciples to Jesus and asked, (Matthew 11:3) "Are You the one who is to come, or shall we look for another?" After all, where was the judgment? Our Lord did plenty of warning, but He wasn't sending anyone to hell.

In answer to John's question, Jesus referred him to the miracles: (Matthew 11:5) "The blind receive their sight and the lame walk, lepers are cleansed and the deaf hear, and the dead are raised up." Then He added, "And the poor have good news preached to them." Thus, Jesus demonstrated His messianic claims by—to use John the Baptist's terminology—"gathering the wheat"; but He was not yet "burning the chaff" (Matthew 3:12). Indeed, even at the end of the Gospel, what did Jesus do? He commissioned the disciples to go out and make more disciples from among all nations by baptizing and teaching (Matthew 28:19–20). The work of final judgment would come later.

But it would come. Other New Testament writers confirm the Baptist's characterization of Jesus as "Judge," and there are many references to Jesus' rendering a future "judgment." In the Gospel of John, for example, our Lord said explicitly that (5:27) "He [the Father] has given Him authority to execute judgment, because He is the Son of Man." In the Book of Acts, Peter identified Him as "the one appointed by God to be judge of the living and the dead" (10:42). Paul also said of Him, "We must all appear before the judgment seat of Christ" (2 Corinthians 5:10) and "Christ Jesus . . . is to judge the living and the dead" (2 Timothy 4:1). In the very last chapter of the New Testament, the Lord Himself says, (Revelation 22:12) "Behold, I am coming soon, bringing My recompense with Me, to repay everyone for what he has done"; and so the faithful pray, (v. 20) "Amen. Come, Lord Jesus!"

4 Judgment Day in the Gospel of Matthew

Christ's second coming for judgment is an especially prominent theme in the Gospel of Matthew. In the Sermon on the Mount, our Lord's first extensive discourse in the book, Jesus spoke a great deal about the end times and judgment. For instance, each of the Beatitudes (Matthew 5:3–12), with which the sermon begins, includes a blessing that the disciples would enjoy fully only after the ending of this age and the coming of the new. The first and the eighth beatitudes (directed to the poor in spirit and the persecuted, respectively) both have the same blessing, "theirs is the kingdom of heaven" (vv. 3, 10). As we have already seen, the "kingdom of heaven" looks forward to the end of time, when God will initiate a new era that removes sin and its consequences from the lives of His people. The other beatitudes each pronounce a future blessing that describes an aspect of the Kingdom. Thus, mourners shall be comforted, the meek shall inherit the earth, those hungry for righteousness shall be satisfied, the merciful shall receive mercy, the pure shall see God, and the peacemakers shall be called sons of God. Christ announces the blessings now, but believers will enjoy them fully only at the end of time.

Elsewhere in the sermon, the theme of judgment occurs in the form of condemnation. Jesus threatens "the hell of fire" for someone who calls his brother a "fool" (v. 22) and declares that salt that loses its taste deserves being thrown out and trampled underfoot (v. 13). It is also in the sermon that we read Jesus' famous remark, (v. 29) "It is better that you lose one of your members than that your whole body be thrown into hell" (also v. 30), directed against those who yield their eyes and hands to sin. Jesus also demands (v. 20) that our "righteousness exceeds that of the scribes and Pharisees" or else "you will never enter the kingdom of heaven."

Divine judgment is also prominent in the final chapter of the sermon (Matthew 7). Those who persist in judging others will themselves be judged (v. 2). Believers are encouraged to follow the "narrow" way that leads to life; but "the gate is wide and the way is easy that leads to destruction" (vv. 13–14). Trees that do not produce "good fruit" are thrown into the fire (v. 19). Then follows a brief description of Judgment Day itself (vv. 21–23), in which Jesus rejects those who call on Him and claim His blessings on account of their impressive works. "Depart from Me, you workers of lawlessness," He tells them. Finally, our Lord concludes with the familiar parable of two foundations, rock and sand (vv. 24–27). Those who build on the latter cannot survive the storms and their house collapses. But who are these? "Everyone who hears these words of Mine [Jesus'] and does not do them." In all these statements, Jesus spoke with authority; condemnation follows those who do not obey His words.

Other words of judgment follow as the Gospel proceeds. Chorazin, Bethsaida, and Capernaum are threatened with a worse condemnation on Judgment Day than the pagan cities of Tyre, Sidon, and Sodom (Matthew 11:22, 24). Judgment Day will include an accounting for one's words (Matthew 12:36–37), but also on that day, the Son of Man will render to every man according to his deeds (Matthew 16:27). Matthew 18 includes warnings against sin in view of the coming judgment (vv. 6, 7–8), and in chapter 19, Jesus tells His disciples that on Judgment Day they too will "sit on twelve thrones, judging the twelve tribes of Israel" (v. 28). In chapter 23, Jesus threatens the scribes and Pharisees with hell (v. 33); and when appearing before Caiaphas, Jesus also tells him, (Matthew 26:64) "From now on you will see the Son of Man seated at the right hand of Power and coming on the clouds of heaven."

Many of the parables in Matthew also point to judgment in connection with the Kingdom; such as the parables of the weeds (Matthew 13:24-30, 36-43), the net (Matthew 13:47–50), and the ten virgins (Matthew 25:1–13). Clearly, Judgment Day is a major theme in the first Gospel.

5 The Final Reckoning

The most detailed description of our Lord's final judgment over mankind occurs in the last of Jesus' great discourses in the Gospel, Matthew 25:31–46. It begins with still another statement that our Lord will return: (v. 31) "When the Son of Man comes in His glory." Accompanied by the angels, the Lord will sit in judgment upon every human being who has ever existed. However, since He separates them into two groups right from the beginning, this scene represents a public announcement of a decision already made. Since God knows the secrets of our hearts (Psalm 44:21), His judgment is long past by Judgment Day, but that is when He will make His verdict public.

Initially, Jesus calls Himself "the Son of Man" in this discourse. He used this term often as a self-designation (around eighty times in the Gospels). Besides reminding us of His human nature, in which He will suffer for the sins of mankind (Matthew 20:28), this term also points to the exalted Savior, who will return in glory to bring the present order of things to an end (this is seen in passages such as Daniel 7:13–14 and Mark 13:24–27). However, besides "Son of Man," the text also calls Jesus "King" (Matthew 25:34, 40) and portrays Him as such ("He will sit on His glorious throne"; v. 31). As we have already seen, "the kingdom of heaven" in the Gospels often points to Judgment Day; and in these verses, we see the king of heaven rendering that final judgment.

Two groups stand before the King. One is placed in the position of privilege (the right) and is designated "sheep"; the other stands on the left and is called "goats." In real life, these animals could be pastured together but could not breed together and would probably be separated for milking, shearing, and other purposes. In the Old Testament, a scapegoat was sent into the wilderness on the Day of Atonement as a symbol of removing sin and guilt (Leviticus 16:7–9). But in this description of judgment, the "goats" remain in their sins and so are sent into hell (v. 41) while the "sheep" represent the heirs of heaven (v. 34). They are two mutually exclusive groups, and there is no third group. It's either one or the other.

The basis for the King's public verdict is the presence or absence of works of mercy in the lives of those gathered before Him. One should not understand this passage as contradicting other passages that ascribe forgiveness of sins to faith in Jesus; for instance, John 3:16 ("God so loved the world") or Romans 3:28 ("One is justified by faith apart from works of the law"). Indeed, it is in Matthew—the same Gospel account that contains the judgment scene—that Jesus' name is explained (1:21: "He will save His people from their sins"), that He institutes the Lord's Supper (26:28: "My blood of the covenant, which is poured out for many for the forgiveness of sins"), and that He defines His saving work (20:28: "the Son of Man came . . . to give His life as a ransom for many").

But our Lord's work of redemption does not leave people unchanged. It transforms them. So when people become believers, they have new attitudes toward God and man, with the result that they do good works spontaneously—not to earn anything but out of gratitude to God their Savior. This is what our Lord refers to in the description of Judgment Day. God's mercy produces mercy in the lives of the faithful; and at Judgment Day, our Lord passes over the sins of the faithful and remembers only their deeds of kindness directed toward others. Out of pure grace—there is no hint of merit—He identifies Himself as the recipient of such deeds and invites believers into the Kingdom prepared for them from the beginning of time.

Six such works are mentioned in Matthew 25—feeding the hungry, giving drink to the thirsty, clothing the naked, taking in strangers, visiting the sick, and visiting the imprisoned. Of course, this is not a complete list of what God expects from His people. Elsewhere in the Gospel, for example, Jesus mentions forgiving a brother's sins (18:21–22) as well as keeping the commandments in general (19:17–19). We are also to make disciples of all nations by baptizing and teaching (28:19–20). But it is also true that as long as they are in this world, people experience physical needs of all kinds, and our Lord wants us to respond to those needs in others. As James reminds us, it is not enough simply to say to the needy, (James 2:16) "Go in peace, be warmed and filled, without giving them the things needed for the body." God expects action, not just words or good intentions. The judgment scene makes this abundantly clear.

Again as James points out, those who fail to respond in love to the needs of others show that their "faith" is not real faith at all: (James 2:17) "Faith by itself, if it does not have works, is dead." Faith saves only because it relies on Jesus; but such a faith always produces good effects. Thus, the second group gathered in front of the King demonstrates its lack of faith by its lack of works. Their condemnation follows inevitably and automatically. Indeed, they condemn themselves.

Conclusion

God's judgment is final and permanent: (Matthew 25:46) "These will go away into eternal punishment, but the righteous into eternal life." Sometimes we act as if time is infinite and will never run out. So we put off telling our friends, neighbors, or loved ones about Jesus. We may even delay dealing with our own personal and pet sins as if we had all the time in the world to do so. But the Bible is really quite clear. Now is the time for repentance and faith—not next year, next month, or next week. Even tomorrow may well be too late.

Christ is coming back. As believers, we can hardly wait! We are righteous because Christ has bestowed His righteousness upon us in our Baptism. He names us as His dearly loved people. Our Lord is returning to gather us up into His everlasting kingdom—so great is His love and mercy and faithfulness toward us! No promise in the Scriptures is more important than this one. We can be absolutely certain of Christ's return for our salvation.

Concluding Activities

Conclude the session with an appropriate prayer and distribute the study leaflet for week 6.

Resurrection

1 Corinthians 15:35–49

Preparing for the Session

Central Focus

This lesson emphasizes two things: (1) the importance of the resurrection of the body for the Gospel, which is a doctrine of immense comfort—without it, Christianity is no longer Christianity; and (2) the biblical basis for this doctrine in both the Old and New Testaments.

Objectives

That participants, led by the Holy Spirit working through God's Word, will

1. understand the biblical basis for the doctrine of the resurrection;
2. realize that since our Lord's resurrection came first, ours shall surely follow at the end of time; and
3. appreciate the hope and comfort that the resurrection of the body offers believers in the face of death—that of loved ones and also their own.

Note for the small-group leaders: Lesson notes and other materials you will need begin on page 69.

For the Lecture Leader

Session Plan

Worship

Begin the session with the hymn printed in the study leaflet. Accompaniments are available in denominational hymnals, such as *Lutheran Service Book* or *Lutheran Worship* (refer to hymnal index). (Note: Concordia Publishing House has available *The Concordia Organist.* All the initial worship hymns in the LifeLight courses are included in this resource. It's especially helpful for mission congregations and small parishes. See the list of study resources on page 7.) Follow with this prayer:

Prayer

Almighty Father, Lord of life and death, strengthen our faith in Your promises of life and resurrection. In the face of temptations to doubt Your Word, send Your Holy Spirit into our hearts through that Word so that we may believe more firmly Your promise that, just as Jesus arose from the dead in triumph, so too You will grant to us glorified bodies at the end of time. For the sake of the same Jesus Christ, our Lord and Savior. Amen.

Lecture Presentation

1 Introduction

When you're dead, you're dead. Right? No, wrong!

But it sure looks that way. If you've ever seen a dead person, you know how permanent death seems. Sometimes at a death, medical people work desperately—frantically—to keep death at bay, but they fail. Everything stops—heartbeat, brain waves, everything—and the person is pronounced dead. We can call or shout; we can weep and cry. It doesn't matter. A dead person no longer hears, no longer speaks, no longer responds. It appears that death is the end, the absolute end.

And yet, when a Christian funeral is reaching its conclusion, what does the pastor say? Standing over the casket right at the graveside, he announces, "We now commit the body . . . to the ground; earth to earth, ashes to ashes, dust to dust, in the sure and certain hope of the resurrection to eternal life through our Lord Jesus Christ" (*LSB Pastoral Care Companion* [Concordia, 2007], p. 134). In the face of death, Christians defy it: "I believe in the resurrection of the body."

2 Promises

What is going on here? Every experience that we have with death certainly looks final. That's why the death of a loved one is so terrible—the loss, the absence, the permanence. It just can't be undone. And yet, as Christians, we insist not only that death can be reversed but that it will be reversed at the end of time on Judgment Day, for this is the promise of Jesus!

The Bible is filled with promises—forgiveness of sins, heaven, and eternal life among them. But none is more important than resurrection. Here's why. Death is the penalty for sin (Romans 6:23: "The wages of sin is death"). Therefore, if death remains the last and final destiny for sin-filled humanity instead of resurrection, then sin has triumphed. It's still there to damn and punish us. No matter how long or intensely Jesus suffered on the cross for our sins, if nonetheless the penalty for our sins remains fixed and permanent, we are headed to the tomb—period. No exceptions and no escape! Then the work of Christ was futile, pointless, vain, and empty.

But that's not the way it was. Christ has won, not sin and not death. So the resurrection is the victory—both His and ours.

No wonder then that the resurrection of the body at the end of time is a principal theme in biblical Christianity. Paul discusses this doctrine at length in both 1 Corinthians 15 and 1 Thessalonians 4, but it is present in many other places as well, not least of all in the teaching of Jesus. There are also references to resurrection in the Old Testament, and Jesus Himself taught that God's announcement to Moses (Exodus 3:6, 15) that He was the God of Abraham, Isaac, and Jacob presupposed the resurrection, for "He is not God of the dead, but of the living, for all live to Him" (Luke 20:37–38). In other words, since only living people can "have a God," Abraham, Isaac, and Jacob must still be alive. Their souls are with God and their bodies will be raised.

Resurrection is indicated in Old Testament passages like Psalm 17:15 ("When I awake, I shall be satisfied with Your likeness") and Isaiah 26:19 ("Your dead shall live; their bodies shall rise"). Daniel 12:2 actually describes the resurrection on Judgment Day: "Many of those who sleep in the dust of the earth shall awake, some to everlasting life, and some to shame and everlasting contempt." And Paul quotes Hosea 13:14 ("O Death, where are your plagues? O Sheol, where is your sting?") at the climax of his great chapter on the resurrection (1 Corinthians 15).

One of the best-known passages of those that teach the resurrection is Job 19:25–27: "I know that my Redeemer lives, and at the last He will stand upon the earth. And after my skin has been thus destroyed, yet in my flesh I shall see God, whom I shall see for myself, and my eyes shall behold, and not another." Death is synonymous with decay, but even so, Job does not hesitate to affirm that he will see God in his flesh; that is, in the very same body in which he died but has now been revived and made alive again.

Job's confession provides an excellent answer to skeptics who raise objections to resurrection based on what happens to a body after death. Decay and corruption set in right away so that the body gradually disappears. Sometimes the body degrades quite rapidly. Think of a cremation, for example. The physical elements have either gone up in smoke or else turned into ashes that can be scattered to the wind. What then?

Well, as Job realized, the destruction of his skin in death—or of any other body part or, indeed, of the entire corpse—is no obstacle to the Creator. He who made Adam out of dust and Eve out of Adam's rib will not be deterred from raising the dead. His Word is what counts, and that Word promises resurrection.

3 Resurrection and Judgment

In the New Testament, resurrection promises are more prominent than in the Old, and they are tied directly to the work of Jesus. To begin with, resurrection is implicit in various descriptions of Judgment Day, such as Matthew 25:32 ("Before Him will be gathered all the nations") and Revelation 1:7 ("Behold, He is coming with the clouds, and every eye will see Him, even those who pierced Him"). If "every" eye will see Him and if "all" the nations of the earth will be there, certainly they must first have been brought back to life. More than once, therefore, Paul reminded his readers that "we must all appear before the judgment seat of Christ" (2 Corinthians 5:10). Since Christ is going to judge everybody, all the dead must rise.

In addition to being a logical necessity in view of Judgment Day, the resurrection of the body on the Last Day is also the explicit teaching of the New Testament. In the Gospel of John (5:28–29), Jesus speaks quite plainly: "An hour is coming when all who are in the tombs will hear His voice and come out, those who have done good to the resurrection of life, and those who have done evil to the resurrection of judgment." "His voice" in this passage refers to the Son of God, Jesus Himself, to whom the Father has turned over the task of final judgment: (v. 22) "The Father judges no one, but has given all judgment to the Son." Therefore, Jesus describes the Father's plan: (6:40) "Everyone who looks on the Son and believes in Him should have eternal life" and then promises, "and I will raise him up on the last day."

Clearly, the resurrection of the dead is closely related to the final judgment. In John 5:29, our Lord actually speaks of two different resurrections, "the resurrection of life" and "the resurrection of judgment." This reflects that what happens on the Last Day is what God has already determined regarding the fate of everyone. The resurrection leads to God's public declaration of what He has already decided—eternal life or eternal damnation. As the final judgment begins, there are already two groups. Obviously, this is good news for some but just the opposite for others.

The final judgment, following the resurrection, applies to all, for God has decided upon one of two eternal destinies for every human being. Paul confessed before Felix, Roman Governor of Judea, (Acts 24:14–15) "I worship the God of our fathers, . . . having a hope in God . . . that there will be a resurrection of both the just and the unjust." He also wrote to the Corinthians, (2 Corinthians 5:10) "We must all appear before the judgment seat of Christ, so that each one may receive what is due for what he has done in the body [i.e., when alive, before death], whether good or evil."

Such passages are warnings against sin in this life and its dreadful consequences in the next, as Paul says in Romans 2:5–6: "Because of your hard and impenitent heart you are storing up wrath for yourself on the day of wrath when God's righteous judgment will be revealed. He will render to each one according to his works." These passages are the purest Law and convict every person of sin. Nobody lives guilt-free. But God did not design the Law to lead us into hypocrisy, like the rich young man of Matthew 19 who claimed to have mastered the Law ("All these I have kept"; v. 20), or into despair, like Judas Iscariot, who hanged himself after betraying Jesus (Matthew 27:3–5). Rather, the purpose of such passages is to show us our sin (Romans 3:20) and so drive us to depend on Christ alone for our salvation: (Romans 3:23–24) "For all have sinned and fall short of the glory of God"—that's the Law—"and are justified by His grace as a gift, through the redemption that is in Christ Jesus"—and that is the Gospel!

Through faith in Jesus, who rescued us from sin, death, and devil, we are ready for everything, even the Last Day. The Scriptures speak of our resurrection as good and wonderful. Resurrection leads not to punishment but to life, when we are forgiven in Christ: (Matthew 25:34) "The King will say to those on His right, 'Come, you who are blessed by My Father, inherit the kingdom prepared for you from the foundation of the world.'"

4 Jesus and the Resurrection

For Christians, therefore, the resurrection is an essential part of the Good News that animates and encourages them always but especially when they or their loved ones confront the reality of death. Already during Jesus' earthly ministry, Martha comforted herself at the death of her brother Lazarus with the promise of resurrection. In John 11:24, she said, "I know that he will rise again in the resurrection on the last day"—to which, our Lord responded in an extraordinary way, first by calling Himself "the resurrection and the life" (v. 25) and then by calling on Lazarus to exit the tomb, although he was already four days dead (vv. 43–44)!

Elsewhere in the Gospels, there are more general references to miracles of resurrection. For example, Jesus answered the question of John the Baptist about whether He was the Messiah by pointing to His deeds, among them raising the dead (Matthew 11:5; Luke 7:22). He also included the performance of such miracles in His instructions to the apostles (Matthew 10:8). And besides the raising of Lazarus, the Bible records two other specific resurrections that Jesus performed; that is, the young man of Nain (Luke 7:14–15) and Jairus's daughter (Luke 8:54–55). We even learn that at the time of Jesus' death and resurrection, (Matthew 27:52–53) "many bodies of the saints . . . were raised, and coming out of the tombs . . . appeared to many."

But the capstone of all such accounts by far—and the foundation of our Christian hope for resurrection to life at the end of time—is our Lord's own resurrection from the dead on Easter. His resurrection was not just resuscitation; that is, coming back to the same kind of life again and subject to the same old afflictions. Rather, Jesus' resurrection was also glorification, an embodied existence for sure but totally different from how He had lived before. On the one hand, Jesus was alive in the same body; for instance, He showed the disciples His wounds (John 20:20, 27). He also invited them to touch His body: (Luke 24:39) "For a spirit does not have flesh and bones as you see that I have." And He ate a piece of broiled fish (v. 42). It was the same Jesus, alive again.

At the time of His birth, our Lord had joined Himself to sinful humanity to live humbly under the Law and to experience life as human beings experience it each day in a sin-cursed world. In every way, He was just like us, except for sin. He carried sin as our substitute but did not Himself commit sin: (2 Corinthians 5:21) "For our sake [God] made Him to be sin who knew no sin, so that in Him we might become the righteousness of God." In other words, after humanity had sinned, Christ became human in order to save us.

But when our Lord had completed His work of redemption, He did not cease being a man. Instead, He arose bodily from the grave, still a true human being, and entered a glorified existence. Thus, Jesus revealed Himself in a "glorified" body, one freed from every trace of sin and all the evils that come from sin. He pointed this out to the two disciples whom He joined on the road to Emmaus on Easter afternoon: (Luke 24:26) "Was it not necessary that the Christ should suffer these things and enter into His glory?" Paul later explained: (Romans 6:9–10) "Christ, being raised from the dead, will never die again; death no longer has dominion over Him. For the death He died He died to sin, once for all, but the life He lives He lives to God." So our Lord continues to live and reign according to His glorified humanity: (1 Peter 3:22) "[Jesus Christ] has gone into heaven and is at the right hand of God, with angels, authorities, and powers having been subjected to Him" until He comes again (Matthew 25:31) "in His glory, and all the angels with Him [and] . . . will sit on His glorious throne."

5 The Lord's Resurrection and Ours

So the resurrection of Jesus was transformative with respect to His body, and it is this kind of resurrection that God promises to us: (Philippians 3:20–21) "The Lord Jesus Christ . . . will transform our lowly body to be like His glorious body." Just as He joined us in our lowliness, so now we will join Him in resurrection glory. The apostle Paul wrote, (1 Corinthians 15:20) "Christ has been raised from the dead, the firstfruits of those who have fallen asleep." By Easter, Jesus did not separate Himself from us but rather demonstrated to us exactly what awaits believers at the end of time; namely, a glorious resurrection just like His.

This connection between our Lord's resurrection on Easter and our own at the end of time is the foundation for what Paul teaches in 1 Corinthians 15, his great resurrection chapter. In the first part of the chapter (vv. 1–11), the apostle affirms the resurrection of Jesus. In the second part (vv. 12–34), he affirms the general resurrection at the end of time; and in the third part (vv. 35–49), he describes the resurrection body before finally concluding (vv. 50–58) with a brief (and triumphant) description of the Last Day. Christ's victory over death on Easter leads to our victory at the end of time.

The Church at Corinth had all kinds of problems, not the least of them doctrinal, for some were saying "that there is no resurrection of the dead" (1 Corinthians 15:12). These doubters were simply stating what seemed most reasonable. Death is the end. Bodies decay and disappear, and nobody can stop the process. That meant that preachers like Paul should be honest and tell the people the truth that when you're dead, that's it. You're not coming back. It's over.

But Paul opposed this false doctrine decisively and in a very remarkable way. He did not refer to God's almighty power, nor did he cite proof passages from the Old Testament, nor did he develop some sort of philosophical argument to address the critics. Instead, he brought forward one incontrovertible fact: Jesus had already done it. He was alive, risen from the dead. For Paul and his contemporaries, the question of resurrection was no longer a theoretical one about which humans could speculate, argue, or guess. It was a matter of fact: Jesus had risen from the dead.

Of course, those who were skeptical about resurrection in general were probably skeptical about the resurrection of Jesus. But Paul had an answer for them: check it out. Ask those who actually saw Jesus after He had arisen. The resurrection had witnesses, and Paul mentions several of them here: Peter, the twelve apostles, more than five hundred people at one time (and most of them were still alive), James, and last of all, Paul himself (1 Corinthians 15:3–8). The resurrection was real, and real people—just like us—saw Jesus and actually touched Him.

Through the years, opponents of Christianity have tried to explain away the resurrection, but they can't do it. Right from the beginning, there were those who said that the disciples had stolen the body. But that hardly makes sense when the disciples were cowering behind locked doors for fear of the authorities. Others have suggested mass hallucination, but that can hardly explain so many different appearances of the Lord to different witnesses at different times and locations.

Still others think that it was all a great conspiracy—a lie by the early Christians to acquire a following. But that's ridiculous. Just think of Paul. What did he gain by becoming a Christian? A life of hardship and persecution and finally death (by beheading, according to church tradition). No, there is only one thing that can explain the transformation of Paul from the foremost persecutor of the Church to its foremost advocate. Just one thing: Jesus was alive and had shown Himself to Paul.

And Paul was not the only one. The first disciples were frightened and demoralized by the death of Jesus. But only a few days later, they were boldly preaching and teaching the Gospel; they continued to do so all their lives, even though they faced opposition everywhere—opposition that often led to martyrdom. Nothing but the resurrection of Jesus can account for what happened to these men. Jesus was alive.

Furthermore, our Lord's resurrection was not just some historical fact that made the first Christians feel good. It was and is the basis for the Gospel. Paul explained in 1 Corinthians 15 that without the resurrection, Jesus would be still in the grave and would have lost the battle against sin. That would then mean that the Gospel was a lie and that Christians would be foolish for committing themselves to it. All the sacrifices made by the faithful, including martyrdom, would make no sense at all without the resurrection, first of all Christ's but then also our own.

But since Jesus is alive, then the promise of bodily resurrection is not only possible but has also already happened. Christ our Lord was just the first to rise. All Christians will follow in His footsteps at the end of time.

This means then that God's grace has completely overcome man's sin—all of it, going all the way back to Adam. By God's justice, He imposed the death penalty upon the first human beings on account of their sins—and then upon their descendants who inherited their sinful condition and followed right along in their path. But by God's grace in Jesus, He has overcome all that sin and all that death, so that (1 Corinthians 15:22–23) "as in Adam all die, so also in Christ shall all be made alive. But each in his own order: Christ the firstfruits, then at His coming those who belong to Christ." That's us!

Conclusion

Appearances can be deceiving. I'm sure that we can all acknowledge this as a truth that applies to much of human experience—everything from the make-believe of a modern fantasy movie to the well-dressed and smooth-talking politician who lies to the public in order to cover up his behavior. But we don't say this about death. There the appearances are the reality. No sign of life actually means no life.

But God says otherwise. Not only the appearance of death but also the reality of death is deceiving. It's not the end. That's why the Bible often calls it "a sleep." The dead will rise again!

Lots of people don't believe this—unfortunately—because they look ahead without first of all looking behind to Jesus. His resurrection changed human reality. Because of Him, even when we die, we are heading into life—and resurrection.

Concluding Activities

Conclude the session with an appropriate prayer and distribute the study leaflet for week 7.

The Last Day

Matthew 24:29–31

Preparing for the Session

Central Focus

The purpose of this lesson is to study the Bible for what it says about the very end of time, the Last Day. Students will learn not only what all humanity can expect at the end but also that for believers it will be a Day of Triumph. The Last Day is really a part of the Gospel.

Objectives

That participants, led by the Holy Spirit working through God's Word, will

1. learn about the events of Judgment Day;
2. appreciate that readiness for the end consists of faith in Jesus, not only the world's judge but also our Savior; and
3. find encouragement and hope in the promise of a glorified body.

Note for the small-group leaders: Lesson notes and other materials you will need begin on page 71.

For the Lecture Leader

Session Plan

Worship

Begin the session with the hymn printed in the study leaflet. Accompaniments are available in denominational hymnals, such as *Lutheran Service Book* or *Lutheran Worship* (refer to hymnal index). (Note: Concordia Publishing House has available *The Concordia Organist.* All the initial worship hymns in the LifeLight courses are included in this resource. It's especially helpful for mission congregations and small parishes. See the list of study resources on page 7.) Follow with this prayer:

Prayer

Heavenly Father, as we contemplate the end of time and of the universe, do not permit our hearts to fail us through fear and unbelief. Instead, by Your grace extended to us in Jesus, confirm our faith so that we may look forward to the Last Day as the culmination of Your promises to us in Him—promises of eternal life and glorified bodies in a new heaven and earth! For Jesus' sake we pray. Amen.

Lecture Presentation

1 Introduction

Jesus did not just predict the Last Day. He also described it and gave signs of its coming. But He didn't announce the exact date, so in a certain sense, it will still be a surprise when it happens. Nevertheless, He provided enough information about it so that Christians can look forward to it and be ready when it finally gets here. Jesus will come in glory, accompanied by the hosts of heaven. All people will arise to stand before Him in judgment. Believers will be transformed into glorified bodies like the Lord's; while unbelievers, along with the devil, will take up permanent residence in hell. God will destroy the present universe and create a new one.

We call it Judgment Day, but for the faithful the Last Day is really a Day of Triumph.

2 Our Lord's Description

There are several references to the Last Day in the Scriptures, but the place to begin is with the description provided by Jesus Himself. In each of the four Gospel accounts, Jesus says something about the Last Day, but His most extensive remarks are in Matthew. Chapters 24 and 25 of the first Gospel constitute our Lord's description of the end times and of the Last Day. Most of this material concerns preparation for that day and focuses especially on the "signs." But these chapters also include the judgment scene that we examined earlier in this series (Lesson 5: Judgment Day). They also provide a brief description of the day itself. Jesus talks about the desperate situation of the faithful during the end times (24:21–28) and the presence of false christs and false prophets before finally getting to the Final Day (Matthew 24:29–31):

Immediately after the tribulation of those days, the sun will be darkened, and the moon will not give its light, and the stars will fall from heaven, and the powers of the heavens will be shaken. Then will appear in heaven the sign of the Son of Man, and then all the tribes of the earth will mourn, and they will see the Son of Man coming on the clouds of heaven with power and great glory. And He will send out His angels with a loud trumpet call, and they will gather His elect from the four winds, from one end of heaven to the other.

When the end comes, we'll know it. The universe itself will begin to collapse, for God will suspend all the rules that He has used for maintaining it; God has maintained it in spite of the fact that human beings have corrupted virtually everything in it over the centuries, even going so far as to worship sun, moon, and stars instead of the Creator. But all that will be over, because God is coming to set all things right again.

Indeed, everyone will see Him. It will be so different from our Lord's first coming! Then, the angels knew what was happening, but as far as humanity was concerned, it was the world's greatest secret. Mary and Joseph, a few shepherds, and foreigners, Wise Men from the East, knew what was happening—and that was it. But not this time! No longer the humble and suffering Servant, Jesus will arrive on the clouds with power and glory. Everyone will know it—all the tribes of the earth, every ethnic group you can think of and all the ones that you don't even know. They will mourn—and why not? Human beings know what they have done and deserve.

But among the many nations, there is still another group, defined not by ethnicity or geography but by repentance and faith. They are called here "His elect." That means that from all eternity God has known and loved them in Christ, made sure that they have heard the Gospel and believed it, and then sustained them in the faith right until the end. Sinners just like everyone else, they are forgiven sinners on account of God's unmerited favor directed to them for the sake of Jesus. Once again, God uses angels, and in a very prominent way—with sound of a trumpet. This time, their task is to gather the elect from all over the globe and so save them from the destruction that is just now arriving. They alone will be ready for the judgment that Matthew recounts in chapter 25.

Our Lord referred to another work of the angels on the Last Day in Matthew 13:41, His explanation to the parable of the weeds: "They will gather out of His kingdom all causes of sin and all law-breakers." Up until the Last Day, the kingdom of God will contain hypocrites, pretenders, people who are probably baptized but are not true believers. At the end of time, God will use angels to root them out.

Implicit but not explicit in Jesus' description in Matthew is the resurrection of the body that will occur on the Last Day. The term "all" in 24:30 and 25:32 admits of no exceptions. In Matthew 12:41–42, Jesus referred to "men of Nineveh" and "the queen of the South" rising up at the Judgment to condemn the generation to which Jesus was preaching. Luke includes a similar saying (11:29–32) and adds another one, a reference to the "resurrection of the just," presumably also on Judgment Day, for Jesus speaks of a reward (Luke 14:14).

John records several references to the resurrection of the dead that place it explicitly on the Last Day; for example, (6:39) "For this is the will of My Father, that I should lose nothing of all that He has given Me, but raise it up on the last day." A more detailed reference occurs in John 5:28–29: "An hour is coming when all who are in the tombs will hear His voice and come out, those who have done good to the resurrection of life, and those who have done evil to the resurrection of judgment."

Through passages like these in the four Gospels, it is clear that our Lord Himself, Jesus Christ, has provided the basis for the Christian teaching regarding the Last Day, Jesus' second coming to raise the dead and render eternal judgment upon all.

3 The Rest of the New Testament

Not surprisingly, the Last Day and final judgment were also important themes in the preaching of the apostles and other first Christians. We find them mentioned in several places in the New Testament. Remember, for example, how the angels appeared at the ascension and promised the second coming: (Acts 1:11) "This Jesus, who was taken up from you into heaven, will come in the same way as you saw Him go into heaven." In the preaching of both Peter and Paul, Jesus is designated as "the one appointed by God to be judge of the living and the dead" (Acts 10:42). Elsewhere, Peter described Jesus as the one who has gone up into heaven "until the time for restoring all the things about which God spoke" (Acts 3:21).

Closely related to Judgment Day—and perhaps even more prominent in early Christian preaching—was the proclamation of resurrection at the end of time. Paul described his faith this way to Governor Felix: (Acts 24:15) "Having a hope in God . . . that there will be a resurrection of both the just and the unjust." Paul also maintained that it was on account of this doctrine that he was in trouble with the authorities, since a leading party of the Jews, the Sadducees, rejected the resurrection: (v. 21) "It is with respect to the resurrection of the dead that I am on trial before you this day." Peter and John suffered persecution from the same group and for the same reason: (Acts 4:1–3) "The priests and the captain of the temple and the Sadducees came upon them, greatly annoyed because they were teaching the people and proclaiming in Jesus the resurrection from the dead. And they arrested them." But Gentiles could also reject this message, as Paul discovered on Mars Hill: (Acts 17:31–32) "'[God] has fixed a day on which He will judge the world in righteousness by a man whom He has appointed; and of this He has given assurance to all by raising Him from the dead.' Now when they heard of the resurrection of the dead, some mocked. But others said, 'We will hear you again about this.'" Thus, Paul's preaching met with either mockery or delay, but in either case, it meant rejection.

Because the second coming was so prominent in the message of the apostles, we find frequent references to Christian anticipations of the Last Day in the New Testament. Just little statements, like when Paul describes the faithful as "waiting for our blessed hope, the appearing of the glory of our great God and Savior Jesus Christ" (Titus 2:13) or "wait[ing] for the revealing of our Lord Jesus Christ, who will sustain you to the end, guiltless in the day of our Lord Jesus Christ" (1 Corinthians 1:7–8), or as having "citizenship . . . in heaven, and from it we await a Savior, the Lord Jesus Christ, who will transform our lowly body to be like His glorious body" (Philippians 3:20).

In view of the end, Peter also described Christians (2 Peter 3:12–13) as "waiting for and hastening the coming of the day of God. . . . But according to His promise we are waiting for new heavens and a new earth in which righteousness dwells." It's no exaggeration to say that in the apostolic Church, a principal characteristic of the first Christians was that they were waiting, expecting, and looking forward to the second coming of Jesus.

Furthermore, there is a lot of information in the epistles that supplements what we learn about the Last Day from the Gospels concerning the resurrection, the final judgment, and the end of the world. For example, Peter provides additional data in chapter 3 of his Second Epistle. And as we saw in the previous lesson, Paul includes a great deal of information about the end in 1 Corinthians 15. He also provides important details regarding the second coming in 1 Thessalonians 4–5.

For example, in 1 Thessalonians 4:13–18, the apostle provides more details regarding the timing of events at the second coming. Paul describes the second coming and elaborates on what our Lord had said earlier in the Gospels about coming in "power and great glory" (Matthew 24:30): (1 Thessalonians 4:16) "The Lord Himself will descend from heaven with a cry of command, with the voice of an archangel, with the sound of the trumpet of God." No one will miss that—not even the dead!

The apostle begins this section by addressing those who were mourning their dead, "those who are asleep" (v. 13)—"asleep"; that is, not gone forever, because those who die in the Lord will come back with the Lord (v. 14) and arise from the dead (v. 16). Obviously, then, not everyone will actually die before the Last Day. Some will still be alive to see what is happening. But all the believers—those still alive as well as those risen again—will greet the Lord as He returns. Paul points out that there is no advantage to still being alive: (vv. 15–17) "We who are alive, who are left until the coming of the Lord, will not precede those who have fallen asleep. . . . The dead in Christ will rise first. Then we who are alive, who are left, will be caught up together with them in the clouds to meet the Lord in the air." What a marvelous scene—all the faithful united with the triumphant Lord forever.

What comes next, of course, is the judgment. Here, too, Paul teaches what Jesus had first taught; namely, that our Lord is coming back in order publicly to render justice upon humanity: (2 Corinthians 5:10) "For we must all appear before the judgment seat of Christ, so that each one may receive what is due for what he has done in the body [i.e., when alive in this life], whether good or evil." Like our Lord's own description in Matthew 25, Paul's also points to works as the evidence for God's judgment: (Romans 2:6, 9–10) "[God] will render to each one according to his works. . . . There will be tribulation and distress for every human being who does evil, . . . but glory and honor and peace for everyone who does good." It is not just the works, however—anybody can pretend to be good by means of works—but rather what the works say about the heart. So Paul writes about (v. 16) "that day when, according to my Gospel, God judges the secrets of men by Christ Jesus." God certainly knows what is going on in every heart, and He will reveal it on the Last Day.

But mentioning works in connection with Christ's judgment at the end of time should not cause us to forget what is central to Paul's understanding of the Gospel: that we are saved through faith alone in Christ the Savior. Indeed, no one can stand before God in judgment apart from Christ, as the apostle points out in the next chapter of Romans: (3:20) "For by the works of the law no human being will be justified in his sight, since through the law comes knowledge of sin." Therefore, we can survive the judgment only "through the redemption that is in Christ Jesus, whom God put forward as a propitiation by His blood, to be received by faith" (vv. 24–25). There is no other way.

4 A Glorified Body

For believers, the Last Day is really a day of triumph, and not the least of the blessings every Christian will receive at that time is a glorified body. Paul is emphatic about this: (1 Corinthians 15:51–52) "Behold! I tell you a mystery. We shall not all sleep [i.e., die], but we shall all be changed, in a moment, in the twinkling of an eye, at the last trumpet. For the trumpet will sound, and the dead will be raised imperishable, and we shall be changed." Instantaneously, therefore, God will transform both the resurrected faithful and those still alive into a new bodily existence, unlike anything experienced previously but just like the bodily existence of the resurrected Jesus.

The apostle compares Adam and our Lord: (1 Corinthians 15:47–49) "The first man was from the earth, a man of dust; the second man is from heaven. As was the man of dust, so also are those who are of the dust, and as is the man of heaven, so also are those who are of heaven. Just as we have borne the image of the man of dust, we shall also bear the image of the man of heaven." Thus, the first man had a natural body formed by God from the dust of the ground (Genesis 2:7) and so, too, have all human beings who were descended from Adam. But at the time of His second coming, the Second Adam, Jesus Christ, will give to believers a spiritual body, physical but imperishable and immortal just like His own imperishable and immortal body.

Since Christ's body is the prototype, we should realize, first of all, that our resurrected body is the same body in which we have lived and died. The disciples saw and touched Jesus after His resurrection, in particular the marks of the nails and of the spear (Luke 24:39–40; John 20:20, 24–29). They knew that it was the Lord. But His body was different—glorified—or as Paul calls it in 1 Corinthians, "a spiritual body" (15:44). This same transformation of our original bodies is what awaits us: (Philippians 3:21) "[Jesus Christ] will transform our lowly body to be like His glorious body."

But what is a glorified body really like? Paul works very hard to help us understand something that is really beyond understanding. He employs a variety of terms and offers analogies to help us grasp in some limited way what our new bodies will be like. For example, Paul helps us to understand the concept of continuity yet transformation in glorified bodies by comparing a corpse to a seed of wheat or some other grain (1 Corinthians 15:35–38). One places the seed into the ground—for all intents and purposes dead—but something wonderful happens. A plant emerges that in form and appearance is totally different from the seed—and yet it originally came from the seed! So, too, our resurrected body will be totally different but still the same body as before.

Paul also reminds us how much variety God employed in the original creation—earthly bodies: humans, animals, birds, and fish; and heavenly: sun, moon, and stars (1 Corinthians 15:38–41). All were different and perfectly so. Such a Creator God will have no difficulty in changing each of us into an appropriate and glorified body on the Last Day.

Using the idea of planting a seed again, Paul uses four short sentences to contrast the body that is planted (in other words, buried) with the body that is raised (1 Corinthians 15:42–44). First, he draws the contrast between "perishable" and "imperishable" (vv. 50, 53–54). On this side of eternity, our bodies don't last. Over time, they get weak, they break down, they malfunction, they die—and in the grave, they decay. But none of this is true any longer in the resurrection. Similarly, in death, our bodies reveal weakness and dishonor—others do whatever they want to us: they dress us or undress us, carry us here or there, and finally dispose of us however they please. But not so our resurrected bodies! Jesus said we would be like "angels in heaven" (Matthew 22:30), no longer subject to sin and its terrible effects, but also no longer constrained by physical desires and needs. Paul describes it as a "spiritual" body, no longer a "natural" one (1 Corinthians 15:44). The struggle with world and devil, the weakness of mortality, the temptations of our own flesh—all that will be over! Instead, we will live in perfect harmony with God, the angels, and all the saints—and in a brand new universe!

5 The End and the Beginning

Besides the resurrection of the body and the final judgment of the living and the dead, the Last Day will also see the destruction of the material universe and its replacement by a new heaven and a new earth. As we have already seen (Matthew 24:29), the failure of sun, moon, and stars is the immediate prelude to our Lord's second coming. A few verses later, Jesus mentions that heaven and earth will "pass away" (v. 35)—as He had also mentioned on other occasions. He also referred to the "close of the age" (Matthew 13:39). But the most complete description of these events is in chapter 3 of Peter's Second Letter.

Peter is answering the scoffers who deny that a final judgment is ever going to come—everything is just the way it has always been (v. 4). Such people, Peter advises, would do well to remember how God already destroyed the world once by means of water, but today "the heavens and earth that now exist are stored up for fire, being kept until the day of judgment and destruction of the ungodly" (v. 7).

We may think that God is needlessly delaying the end; but God is not like us—and thankfully so—since His apparent "slowness" is the result of His patience with sinners. God wants no one to perish, and so He is giving the world time for people to repent (v. 9). Nevertheless, that Last Day will come, (v. 10) "and then the heavens will pass away with a roar, and the heavenly bodies will be burned up and dissolved."

Wow! The mind "boggles" just to think about such destruction. But if we find that hard to imagine, how much less can we conceive of that which follows: (v. 13) "We are waiting for new heavens and a new earth in which righteousness dwells." Only God knows what the new universe will be like, but we can be sure it will be wonderful.

Conclusion

God has told us a lot about the Last Day, but not everything. Even as we conclude this lecture, we probably have many questions that remain unanswered about what will happen then and what our new lives will be like. However, the apostle John provides a good way of bringing such concerns to an end. He writes: (1 John 3:2) "Beloved, we are God's children now, and what we will be has not yet appeared; but we know that when He appears we shall be like Him, because we shall see Him as He is."

We don't need to know everything. Indeed, just one thing is necessary—to know that we are God's children. This is what Jesus taught and made possible through His death and resurrection. It's also what God has granted us in Baptism. Therefore, we have every confidence that when the Last Day arrives, we will be ready for all the wonderful things that God has in store for us.

Concluding Activities

Conclude the session with an appropriate prayer and distribute the study leaflet for week 8.

Signs of the Times
Matthew 24:3–28

Preparing for the Session

Central Focus

The main purpose of this lesson is to familiarize the student with the signs that the Bible gives to remind us that Christ will really come back to judge the living and the dead. These signs occur in nature, society, and the Church. Many people—including church people—refuse to believe that the world will end the way the Bible says, but the signs say otherwise. People need to be ready.

Objectives

That participants, led by the Holy Spirit working through God's Word, will

1. learn about the signs of the end times that Jesus described to His disciples;
2. learn about the signs that are described elsewhere in the New Testament other than the Gospels; and
3. appreciate God's goodness in providing such signs so as to keep believers' faith focused on the promises associated with the second coming of Jesus.

Note for the small-group leaders: Lesson notes and other materials you will need begin on page 73.

For the Lecture Leader

Session Plan

Worship

Begin the session with the hymn printed in the study leaflet. Accompaniments are available in denominational hymnals, such as *Lutheran Service Book* or *Lutheran Worship* (refer to hymnal index). (Note: Concordia Publishing House has available *The Concordia Organist*. All the initial worship hymns in the LifeLight courses are included in this resource. It's especially helpful for mission congregations and small parishes. See the list of study resources on page 7.) Follow with this prayer:

Prayer

Heavenly Father, open our minds so we may better understand the signs of the times that the Bible describes to prepare us for the end of the world. As we see such signs in the contemporary world, strengthen our faith in Jesus' promises to return again and to take the faithful to be with Him forever in a new heaven and a new earth. Please hear us for Jesus' sake. Amen.

Lecture Presentation

1 Introduction

Resurrection. Judgment. The end of the world. Pretty important stuff, I'd say, and I'd like to be ready for them. How about you?

But it's hard to maintain readiness and keep focused on the end when one day just follows the next and we don't seem to be any closer to the second coming than we were before. Of course, we are deceiving ourselves, since time is marching on to its end. It just doesn't seem that way.

So maybe we ought to take another look and try to see things from a biblical perspective. In order to help us stay ready for the Last Day, the Scriptures have identified several "signs" of the end times—things in nature, society, and the Church that teach us that the end is near. Our Lord could come at any moment.

2 Jesus' Discourse about the End

As we have seen before, the Lord addressed the issues that interest us about the end times in Matthew 24 and 25. That is especially true of the signs of the times, since Jesus' discourse on these topics actually began in answer to a question from the disciples: (Matthew 24:3) "Tell us, when will these things be, and what will be the sign of Your coming and of the close of the age?" You see, the disciples also wanted to be ready, so they asked the right questions: when and what sign?

Right away, however, we face a challenge in understanding Jesus' answer because He and the disciples are talking about two things at once: the destruction of Jerusalem and the second coming. But it is also true that the first is a foreshadowing of the second. Just as God's patience with the sins of the chosen people finally ran out and He punished them by the destruction of Jerusalem and the temple at the hands of the Romans in AD 70, so God's patience with the sins of humanity will finally exhaust itself and our Lord will return in judgment. So the description of the first blends easily into a description of the second.

As Jesus answers the disciples, He does not always distinguish sharply between the two, but 24:4–14 seems to discuss the end of the world, verses 15–22 the destruction of Jerusalem, and verses 23–31 the second coming. However, much of what Jesus says about preparing for the end of Jerusalem is also relevant to being ready for the end of time.

When our Lord was bringing His earthly ministry to an end, He reflected on the failure of God's chosen people to respond in faith to Him and to His message. Although there were exceptions, the majority of the Jewish leadership rejected Him and connived at His death (Matthew 26:3–4). So Jesus wept over Jerusalem and predicted its demise (23:37–38).

Perhaps in response to Jesus' solemn words, the disciples later called His attention to the magnificent buildings that constituted the temple in Jerusalem; but our Lord repeated His prediction even more clearly: (Matthew 24:2) "Truly, I say to you, there will not be left here one stone upon another that will not be thrown down." When the leaders and the people determined to reject Jesus, they sealed their own fate. God's judgment would strike, through the pagan Romans, about forty years later. Then the troops of Titus (later to become emperor) besieged and overran the city, slaughtered thousands, burned many of the buildings, and destroyed the temple.

Our Lord's prediction caused some discussion, we can be sure, so the disciples pursued the topic by asking for a sign. To them, the destruction of Jerusalem and the end of the age were closely united (if not one and the same!), so they inquired about both. And Jesus answered by discussing both.

3 Jesus Describes the Signs

It is noteworthy that the first sign that Jesus mentions is false christs: (Matthew 24:5) "For many will come in My name, saying, 'I am the Christ,' and they will lead many astray." In verses 23 and 24, He elaborates on how bad it will be: false christs and false prophets will deceive many by performing "great signs and wonders"—lying miracles, no less! There never has been a time when the Church has not experienced such charlatans, especially when we realize that false christs are not only those who claim to be Christ Himself but also those who claim falsely to speak in His name. The latter are often more devious than the former. They look good, they sound right, they sometimes help people with their temporal needs, and they offer answers to the problems that plague us, but what they say leads us away from God and not toward Him. Their words are not true. Already in the Sermon on the Mount, Jesus warned against them: (Matthew 7:15) "Beware of false prophets, who come to you in sheep's clothing but inwardly are ravenous wolves."

But how do we recognize them? Jesus says, (Matthew 7:16) "You will recognize them by their fruits," but what are the fruits of a false prophet? Since the task of a true prophet is to speak God's Word, the "fruit" of a false one is his false speaking—that is, his false teachings. Only a real familiarity with the Scriptures can prepare one for this. Christians must learn to discern truth from lies by comparing what is taught to the Scriptures. Any other standard, such as "humility," "sincerity," or "charisma," leads to the deception that Jesus is warning against.

If Jesus, however, was already warning the people of His own day against spokesmen who falsely claim to represent Him, how can false christs be a sign of the end times? This is also a question concerning the signs that Jesus mentions in Matthew 24:6–7: "Wars and rumors of wars. . . . nation will rise against nation, and kingdom against kingdom." Has there ever been a time this has not been true? Similarly, the next two signs: "famines and earthquakes." We read and hear about such things all the time, and in fact, Jesus Himself said with respect to the conflict between nations, "this must take place, but the end is not yet" and with respect to the natural disasters, "these are but the beginning." So what does our Lord mean by calling them "signs"?

Just this: God wants us to know from experience that we live in a fallen world. Something is not right with a world characterized by "prophets" who lead people to hell or by human suffering caused either by nature (earthquakes and famines) or by people (warfare). Is it right that the weakest, poorest, least-able members of society often are the ones who suffer most at such times? And yet we know from our Lord's work and words that God is a loving Father. So He will not permit such wicked things to go on forever. They are going to end. The goodness of God demands it. Therefore, they function as a perpetual reminder to everyone to get ready for the end. Now is the time to do it, not tomorrow, but now.

The next signs (Matthew 24:9–14) are specific to the Christian Church; first of all persecution: (v. 9) "They will deliver you up to tribulation and put you to death, and you will be hated by all nations for My name's sake." Of course, this is exactly how His opponents treated Jesus. So can Christians expect anything less? Furthermore, this is one way—and a very effective way—that Christians can witness to others about the power and life-changing character of Christianity. Often, persecution provides opportunities for confession, as with Peter and John before the Jewish Council (Sanhedrin; Acts 4:5–12) or Paul before Agrippa (Acts 26:2–23), and it always offers examples of patience and charity, since we know (2 Corinthians 4:17) that "this light momentary affliction is preparing for us an eternal weight of glory beyond all comparison."

Nevertheless, we must not be naïve. Jesus also warns that persecution works. Not everyone is willing to become a martyr, "and then many will fall away" (Matthew 24:10). To this, He adds that false prophets will "lead many astray" (v. 11) and, finally, that with the increase of lawlessness (immorality of every sort) at the end, "the love of many will grow cold" (v. 12). Thus, the institutional church, consisting of those who claim to be Christian, will undergo persecution on the outside and apostasy within. In fact, so bad will it become that Jesus even says—with respect to the destruction of Jerusalem but certainly applicable to the end as well—(Matthew 24:22) "If those days had not been cut short, no human being would be saved. But for the sake of the elect those days will be cut short."

Although persecution is a constant in the history of the Church, it will intensify toward the end. In fact, Jesus calls it "great tribulation, such as has not been from the beginning of the world until now, no, and never will be" (Matthew 24:21). However, we need to know that no matter how bad it looks or feels, God is still ultimately in charge. He will not permit the "elect," that is, the ones whom He has known and loved in Christ from all eternity, to fall away. Elsewhere, God promises that He will not let believers be tempted above what they can bear but will instead provide a way of escape (1 Corinthians 10:13). Indeed, Christ promises the ultimate escape from the intense persecution of the last days: "Immediately after the tribulation of those days," the end will come (Matthew 24:29–31).

Besides persecution, however, Jesus tells of another sign in the Church of an entirely opposite character: (Matthew 24:14) "And this gospel of the kingdom will be proclaimed throughout the whole world as a testimony to all nations, and then the end will come." Here we have what is perhaps the most important reason for our Lord's "delaying" His return—to let the Gospel go out until it reaches the last possible person who will hear and believe it. Only God knows who that will be, and He will not permit the end until that happens. The Gospel must be preached!

As with the other signs, however, so too with this one: We do not know precisely when God will fully accomplish it. But we are not supposed to! God has not given these signs so that we can calculate precisely when the Last Day will arrive. In fact, Jesus warns against even trying: (Matthew 24:36) "But concerning that day and hour no one knows, not even the angels of heaven, nor the Son, but the Father only." This is why, therefore, Paul describes Judgment Day as arriving like "a thief in the night" (1 Thessalonians 5:2).

In spite of the signs, therefore, the world will not be ready for the end when it comes. Instead, everything will seem quite ordinary. Jesus compares the situation to the days before Noah's flood: (Matthew 24:38–39) "They were eating and drinking, marrying and giving in marriage, until the day when Noah entered the ark, and they were unaware until the flood came and swept them all away." So too the second coming! All at once, it will happen, and the separation for judgment will begin: (Matthew 24:40–41) "Two men will be in the field; one will be taken and one left. Two women will be grinding at the mill; one will be taken and one left."

The world expects everything to continue just the way it is, but we need to be ready for the end. We need to pay attention to the signs.

4 "Signs of the Times" in Paul's Letters

Jesus' apostles taught the need to be ready for the end, just like their Master. Peter, for example, wrote, (2 Peter 3:14) "Since you are waiting for these [the new heavens and a new earth], be diligent to be found by Him without spot or blemish, and at peace." John also warned, (1 John 2:28) "Abide in Him, so that when He appears we may have confidence and not shrink from Him in shame at His coming." This is true also of Paul. In fact, in his two letters to the Thessalonians, Paul had occasion both to reaffirm the resurrection of the body at the end of time in his first one and to discuss the signs of the end in the second.

In the first letter, Paul stressed the necessity for constant readiness, given the suddenness with which the Last Day would arrive: (1 Thessalonians 5:3) "While people are saying, 'There is peace and security,' then sudden destruction will come . . . and they will not escape." But this should not be true of the faithful: (v. 4) "You are not in darkness, brothers," writes the apostle, "for that day to surprise you like a thief." Instead, Paul urges, (v. 8) "Let us be sober, having put on the breastplate of faith and love, and for a helmet the hope of salvation." In other words, we can be ready for the last days when we live by faith, hope, and love; and God will not let us down: (v. 9) "For God has not destined us for wrath, but to obtain salvation through our Lord Jesus Christ."

In the second letter, Paul had to address an error apparently circulating among the Thessalonians; namely, that the "day of the Lord" had already come (2 Thessalonians 2:2)! So, in the first chapter, Paul describes what that day will really be like. He does so in connection with the current sufferings of the Thessalonian Christians. On Judgment Day, God will "repay with affliction" those who have afflicted the faithful (2 Thessalonians 1:6). God will save the believers, but those who reject the Gospel "will suffer the punishment of eternal destruction" (v. 9).

In the following chapter, Paul introduces another sign of the times that must be fulfilled before the end comes: the appearance of "the man of lawlessness" (1 Thessalonians 2:3). This person is often called "the Antichrist." John uses this term in his epistles, first of all, for all the false christs of which Jesus had spoken—all those who use the name of Christ to teach contrary to God's Word; but he also speaks of the Antichrist, "which you heard was coming and now is in the world already" (1 John 4:3). This is the one of whom Paul is speaking in 2 Thessalonians.

Since the Middle Ages, many Christians have identified the Antichrist with the Roman Catholic papacy on account of the pope's fulfilling of the apostle's description. First of all, the papacy claims to be the "vicar of Christ" and declares with the authority of Christ teachings that contradict the Bible—everything from the immaculate conception of the Virgin Mary to opposition to capital punishment (2 Thessalonians 2:4). Then, too, the papacy supports its claims with "false signs and wonders" (2 Thessalonians 2:9)—just think of the "miracles" with which the papacy determines who is a saint and appoints a place in heaven to people like Pius V and Robert Bellarmine, both of whom devoted themselves to opposing the Reformation. But most important, there is its "wicked deception for those who are perishing, because they refused to love the truth and so be saved" (2 Thessalonians 2:10). Even today, the papacy promotes doctrines like the cult of the saints (such as prayers to Mary) and burdens consciences with unscriptural laws (such as the celibacy of the clergy). Such abuses do not come from God but from the devil (cf. 1 Timothy 4:1–3). Nevertheless, the papacy promotes them in the name of Christ. Thus, they are signs of the Antichrist that Christians should not ignore, even if contemporary popes often exhibit admirable personal qualities and speak correctly on some issues, like abortion.

"Antichrist" and all the other signs mentioned in the teachings of Jesus and His apostles have but one basic purpose: to prepare us for the end. We need to be ready.

5 Millennialism

Besides all the signs already mentioned, some people have also wanted to interpret the last book of the New Testament, the Book of Revelation, as a kind of road map for Church history from beginning to end, just filled with prophetic signs of the times. This is not the best approach. As one soon realizes upon reading it, Revelation is—at least after the first few chapters—a book of symbolic word-pictures in which fantastic figures participate in cosmic events, different from anything that anyone experiences literally. Such visions demand interpretation. But how do we do that?

The best answer—and always a good rule for biblical interpretation—is to let the clear teachings of Scripture interpret the dark passages. In the case of Revelation, that would mean that we use the rest of the New Testament, especially those books that best present the work and significance of our Lord, to help us understand the visions that John describes. We cannot be dogmatic; interpretations can and will vary. After all, symbols and metaphors depend in part on what the reader himself brings to a text. However, we can insist that whatever is put forward as the meaning of a passage in Revelation must not contradict what we know from clear teachings elsewhere.

This brings us to the "millennium." This is an idea about the end times that is taught by many on the basis of Revelation but one that actually conflicts with what we know about the end of the world from the rest of Scripture. So "millennialism" is a whole array of teachings about the end that are spun out from an incorrect understanding, especially of Revelation 20. Unfortunately, these false teachings can lead to confusion and doubt concerning what the Bible really says about the end times and the Christian faith as it looks forward to the end.

There are many kinds and variations of millennialism. The word *millennium* means "a thousand years" and refers to that period of time as mentioned five times in Revelation 20 (vv. 2, 3, 4, 5, 6). The chapter also refers to an angel with "the key to the bottomless pit"; calls Satan a "dragon" whom an angel locks in the pit; talks about worshiping "the beast" and mentions its "mark" on foreheads or hands; and describes the devil, Death, and Hades as being thrown into "the lake of fire." Clearly, such language needs interpreting. So does the thousand years.

But some persist in taking the millennium literally and insist that Christ will return—not at the end of time but a thousand years before the end—in order to establish a visible reign of peace on earth with His capital at Jerusalem. This would also give the Jewish people a second chance to become Jesus' followers. Then, just as the thousand years are ending, there would occur a literal battle between the forces of faith and unbelief, after which the end would finally come.

Now, does any of this fit with what Jesus or Paul actually taught regarding the end times and judgment? As our Lord Himself said, (Matthew 25:31–32) "When the Son of Man comes in His glory, and all the angels with Him, then will He sit on His glorious throne. Before Him will be gathered all the nations, and He will separate people one from another." This is judgment, not kingdom building. Time's up! Now is the time for repentance and faith—and for evangelism. We should not put our hope in a millennium.

Of course, this is just one kind of millennialism. There are several others, but they all include a misreading of Revelation 20. However, if we proceed from what we know about the end times from elsewhere in the Bible, then we can interpret the thousand years correctly. One view that many nonmillennialists find persuasive is that it represents the era of the New Testament Church, during which our Lord permits Christians to take the Gospel all around the world. At the very end of this period, there will be the great tribulation and apostasy that occur just before the second coming. Interpretations like this one do not violate the rest of Scripture—and that's the important thing.

Conclusion

We are living in the last times. Peter announced this already on Pentecost when he maintained that the outpouring of the Spirit on that day was the fulfillment of what the prophet Joel had said: "And in the last days it shall be, God declares" (Acts 2:17). But if you find these words hard to believe, just look at the signs. God, in His grace, has given us signs that will be always before us, reminding us of Christ's imminent return and calling on us to be ready at all times. These signs are all being fulfilled right now as we speak. The end is near. Christ is coming. Amen. Come, Lord Jesus!

Concluding Activities

Conclude the session with an appropriate prayer and distribute the study leaflet for week 9.

So What?

Matthew 24:42–44

Preparing for the Session

Central Focus

The goal of this lesson is to draw out implications for the Christian life from the doctrine of the end times. In particular, this lesson shows that the second coming provides a powerful incentive to remain in the faith and to serve God by serving others. God's promises of life everlasting and resurrection also offer great encouragement to believers when they must experience troubles here.

Objectives

That participants, led by the Holy Spirit working through God's Word, will

1. understand that the doctrine of the end times has direct implications for their faith and life;
2. learn what the Bible has to say about the Christian life in view of the end; and
3. find comfort when they face death in the promises of Christ for believers at the end of time.

Note for the small-group leaders: Lesson notes and other materials you will need begin on page 76.

For the Lecture Leader

Session Plan

Worship

Begin the session with the hymn printed in the study leaflet. Accompaniments are available in denominational hymnals, such as *Lutheran Service Book* or *Lutheran Worship* (refer to hymnal index). (Note: Concordia Publishing House has available *The Concordia Organist.* All the initial worship hymns in the LifeLight courses are included in this resource. It's especially helpful for mission congregations and small parishes. See the list of study resources on page 7.) Follow with this prayer:

Prayer

Heavenly Father, You desire that the seed of Your Word should always bring forth fruit in the lives of those who hear it. Bless us, we pray, with strong faith and commitment to You in our lives now as a result of what we have learned from the Bible about the end times and the promises of eternal blessings at the second coming of Jesus. Through the same Jesus Christ, Your Son and our Lord. Amen.

Lecture Presentation

1 Introduction

So what? That's right—so what? What difference does it make if we are living in the end times? If the second coming, judgment, and resurrection could happen at any moment in the future, that's fine. But how does that affect the here and now? It may be nice to know—after all, the Bible teaches it, and at the funeral of a loved one, ideas of heaven and resurrection are certainly comforting, but do they have any purpose other than that? Do doctrines about the future really affect how we live today?

They certainly should, for the Christian lives life in between two poles—the first coming of Christ, especially His death and resurrection, and His second coming, especially His promises of bodily resurrection and life everlasting. Honest self-examination reminds the Christian of his faults and sins every day. What's the remedy? The work of Christ in the past has reconciled us to the Father and earned for us the forgiveness of our sins. But we also experience physical frailties, the loss of loved ones, and the hostility of the world. What's the remedy for all that? Christ's work in the future will bring about a new heaven and a new earth. That's what we are living for!

2 Watching and Waiting

The importance of living with an eye toward the future comes up almost every time that Jesus speaks of the second coming. One of the ways that Jesus made this point was by urging His disciples to stay awake: (Matthew 24:42, 44) "Therefore, stay awake, for you do not know on what day your Lord is coming. . . . Therefore you also must be ready, for the Son of Man is coming at an hour you do not expect." Of course, we need to explore more closely what our Lord means by "staying awake," but one thing that is clear initially is that Christians need to remain Christian all their lives. No matter what their situation—whether they are hard pressed by circumstances or severely tempted by Satan or even have succumbed and fallen into desperate sin (like David or Peter), they must not give up, for Jesus says, (Matthew 10:22) "The one who endures to the end will be saved"; and again, (Revelation 2:10) "Be faithful unto death, and I will give you the crown of life."

Maybe that's easier said than done—biblical descriptions of the end times can be alarming. After all, who wants to hear about a tribulation so terrible that if God did not shorten those times, "no human being would be saved"! Thank God that our Lord immediately adds that "for the sake of the elect those days will be cut short" (Matthew 24:22). Of course, that word "elect" moves us to look backward again—this time farther than we actually can look! For God's love for us in Christ originated before creation. Paul wrote: (Ephesians 1:4–5) "He chose us in Him before the foundation of the world, that we should be holy and blameless before Him. In love He predestined us for adoption as sons through Jesus Christ." Therefore, on account of His love for us in eternity, God sent His Son into time—a specific time as well as place—in order to redeem us. As God oversees human history, He is always guided by His own gracious purpose to save us. The work of Jesus for our sakes is the proof and fulfillment of His love for us from before the beginning of time.

But the work of Jesus in the past is not the end of God's love for us. It is present right now and guarantees the future. "For the sake of the elect" (Matthew 24:22), God will shorten the great tribulation. Moreover, even as the faithful endure that time of suffering, they know what is coming next—or rather, who is coming: (Matthew 24:29, 30) "Immediately after the tribulation of those days," the universe will collapse and Jesus will appear, and "they will see the Son of Man coming on the clouds of heaven." In this way, even that final period of tribulation becomes a pointer toward the ultimate victory that awaits us in Christ.

And that victory is what will keep us going even during the worst times. After all, through all the centuries of Christian history, God's grace, power, and promises have sustained believers in all kinds of circumstances, including martyrdom. Just think of Stephen, the first martyr and the prototype of all the rest, who not only confessed Jesus right until the end but also died with a prayer on his lips: "Lord, do not hold this sin against them" (Acts 7:60), in imitation of the Savior (Luke 23:34).

3 Patience, Everybody!

So we have God's promises of His love to us in Jesus—yesterday, today, and forever—to keep us in the faith right until the end, even during the worst of times. But what about better times? Things are never perfect, but Christians do not always live under a direct threat of martyrdom. In His goodness, God has often arranged for Christians to go about their daily lives without fear of violence from the state or other powers. At some times and places, Christians have even prospered and become influential in society. But situations like these also have their down side. Peter, for example, mentions the emergence of skeptics who scoff at Christian claims that the end is coming.

The apostle addresses such scoffers in his second letter. Wishing to follow their own sinful desires, these mockers question the second coming with its threat of judgment. "All things are continuing as they were from the beginning of creation" is their claim (2 Peter 3:4). But they fail to look back and recall the flood—the first instance of God's worldwide condemnation of sin (vv. 5–6)—while at the same time denying a future judgment by fire (v. 7).

Peter reminds us that God does not regard time the way we do: (v. 8) "With the Lord one day is as a thousand years." Moreover, there is a reason why Christ has still not returned: (v. 9) "The Lord . . . is patient toward you, not wishing that any should perish, but that all should reach repentance." Nevertheless, God's gracious "delay" must not lead us to join the scoffers, for Christ is coming. "The day of the Lord will come like a thief" (v. 10), says the apostle, but it will come!

It will arrive with a mighty destruction: (v. 7) "The heavens and earth that now exist are stored up for fire, being kept until the day of judgment and destruction of the ungodly" (see also v. 10). But such a reality in the future should affect people right now. Peter draws a conclusion that better helps us to understand what our Lord meant by "stay awake": (vv. 11–12) "What sort of people ought you to be in lives of holiness and godliness, waiting for and hastening the coming of the day of God"! We know that faith always produces good works—not just faith in the past work of Christ but faith in His future work as well. Living with the expectation that the Lord is truly coming back to condemn the wicked but to rescue the faithful changes one's perspective on life. Because of this future, Christians live in God-pleasing ways now, no matter the circumstances, good or bad.

4 Word Pictures

Jesus often referred to the end in word pictures or parables. In fact, two of the parables in Matthew 13—the chapter in which our Lord introduces parables—relate directly to the judgment at the end of time. The second and briefer of these, the parable of the net (vv. 47–50), affirms the fact of judgment and especially the condemnation of the wicked: (vv. 49–50) "The angels will come out and separate the evil from the righteous and throw them into the fiery furnace." The first of these is a little more involved, the parable of the weeds (vv. 24–30), and Jesus offers His own explanation (vv. 36–43). It too affirms Judgment Day but also teaches that judgment is God's business, not ours. The master instructs His servants not to separate the weeds from the wheat but to wait until the harvest. So during this age, we must put up with the wicked (remember: God wants all to be saved); but at the end of time, God will vindicate His own (Matthew 13:41–43):

The Son of Man will send His angels, and they will gather out of His kingdom all causes of sin and all lawbreakers, and throw them into the fiery furnace. In that place, there will be weeping and gnashing of teeth. Then the righteous will shine like the sun in the kingdom of their Father.

By insisting that Judgment Day really will come, our Lord encourages the faithful to keep going. Wickedness may reign now, but God promises that it will end!

Our Lord also incorporated "picture language" into His "end times" discourse in Matthew 24 and 25. For example, in Matthew 24:32–35, our Lord points His disciples to the lesson of the fig tree: (vv. 32–33) "As soon as its branch becomes tender and puts out its leaves, you know that summer is near. So also, when you see all these things, you know that He [the Son of Man] is near, at the very gates." In spite of our doubts, the signs point infallibly to the future second coming. You can be sure of this, Jesus adds, (v. 35) "Heaven and earth will pass away, but My words will not pass away." Thus, we have a very good reason for persevering in the faith. God keeps His Word—both of blessing and of judgment.

Our Lord's final discourse also includes the parable of the ten virgins (Matthew 25:1–13), at the end of which Jesus explains its meaning: (v. 13) "Watch therefore, for you know neither the day nor the hour." The parable is a familiar one. Ten maidens are waiting for the bridegroom to arrive and the marriage celebration to begin, but five are "foolish" and so bring no extra oil along for their lamps. Since the bridegroom is delayed, they run out of oil with which to trim their lamps when he finally arrives. So while they are off trying to buy some, the celebration starts and the foolish virgins are left out. They weren't ready. Thus, the parable admonishes us to be ready!

But how? We get a little better understanding of readiness for the end when Jesus compares His followers to servants who have been entrusted with tasks to carry out while their master is absent. In Matthew 24:45–51, our Lord describes two servants. The first is "faithful and wise" (v. 45) because he carries out his duty all during the master's absence. His special responsibility is to make sure that the master's household has enough food to eat at the right time. That wouldn't be easy, but he does it. So the master rewards him upon his return. That's one picture. The other is completely the opposite. The "wicked" servant exploits his position—beats his fellow servants and lives it up with drunkards—because he thinks the master is delayed. But the master is coming. He returns without advance warning and renders judgment upon the wicked servant to "cut him in pieces" (v. 51)! Clearly, this brief parable makes the point again that we need to be ready, but the behavior of the servants reflects the self-giving ethic that characterizes Jesus' disciples. The faithful servant devotes himself to the household; but the wicked one pursues self-indulgence and cruelty.

In other words, being ready includes doing what God has charged us with doing until the second coming arrives. Obviously, this is still very broad, since every Christian has his own unique situation in which he carries out the vocation into which God has placed him; for instance, as father, mother, son, daughter, husband, wife, single person, employer, or employee. Nevertheless, undergirding every calling is this principle: Love your neighbor as yourself (Galatians 5:14). Christians are supposed to do whatever they do out of care and concern for others. They are not supposed to live selfishly.

God will accept no alternatives to what He has commanded. In the Sermon on the Mount, when Jesus offers a brief description of the final judgment, He condemns those who know His name and claim to have done "mighty works" but really are "workers of lawlessness." "Depart from me," He tells them (Matthew 7:22–23).

There is still another parable that shows the seriousness with which Jesus expects us to carry out our God-given tasks in view of the second coming. It comes immediately after the parable of the ten virgins. This is the parable of the talents (Matthew 25:14–30). In this story, Jesus describes God's judgment as a reckoning between a master and his three servants to whom he had entrusted money for investment. Two of the servants did as commanded and are rewarded, but the third has failed entirely. He buried his money, so the master denounces him as worthless and orders him cast out into "outer darkness."

Again, the message is clear. Waiting for the end means working for the Lord. No excuses. God has entrusted us with remarkable gifts, both temporal and spiritual. But we are not their ultimate owners, only stewards or managers, so the Lord expects us to use them appropriately for the extension of His kingdom. After all, we are not here in order to work our own way to heaven. Christ has accomplished that. We are here to demonstrate the love of God to others. So that's what we do while we wait for the end.

5 In the Face of Death

Besides patient perseverance in doing good while we wait for Christ to come again, His second coming brings blessings to believers right now! When we consider the significance of Christ's promises regarding the end of the world, we should never minimize the comfort that they bring, especially when confronting death—and first of all, the death of loved ones.

In an earlier lesson, we considered what the Bible has to say about heaven. This is basic to our living through the loss of one whom we love. "Today you will be with Me in Paradise"—our Lord's word to the thief on the cross—is something that we hold on to when a loved one dies, perhaps by slipping away into eternity after a long illness or maybe by being torn from our grasp through a sudden catastrophe. Either way, we can rejoice that something good awaits a believer whom we are mourning. We don't have to worry about those who die in the faith.

However, we cannot even imagine what this good thing is (heaven) without also imagining bodies—perhaps light and airy ones, but still bodies. We think of our loved ones singing God's praises or renewing acquaintances with family and friends or making new ones of biblical or historical figures. But these activities take bodies—at least as far as we can tell. Of course, we never want to impose the limitations of our imaginations on God. He can certainly create a paradise for disembodied souls. But, in point of fact, our thinking of loved ones still with their bodies is not all wrong. For God has promised not only heaven but also the resurrection of the body in the future in connection with the second coming of Jesus.

So precisely at funerals, when we are comforting ourselves with the thought of our loved ones in heaven and we imagine them in new and restored bodies, healed from all the ravages of time, illness, and sin, those imaginings have a foundation in the future work of Jesus Christ, "who will transform our lowly body to be like His glorious body" (Philippians 3:21).

God's promise of a glorified body at end of the time is the source of immense comfort and strength when we face life without someone we love. It may be sad, challenging, difficult, almost impossible—but not permanent. Remember Paul's description of the Last Day: (1 Thessalonians 4:16–17) "The dead in Christ will rise first. Then we who are alive, who are left, will be caught up together with them in the clouds to meet the Lord in the air, and so we will always be with the Lord." And then he adds, (v. 18) "Therefore encourage one another with these words." That's the point. The promise of a final resurrection provides comfort and encouragement for those of us who are alive now. We know that a restoration and reunion awaits all those who themselves are waiting for Jesus.

But it's not only others whose death we have to deal with; it's also ourselves. We too must die—and we know it. The younger and healthier we are, the more we can ignore it, and most of us do just that—ignore death. But we can't do it all the time. Not only do obituaries and funerals occasionally put the thought of dying into our heads but life itself also provides intimations of mortality. A narrow escape from an accident, for example, prompts us to exclaim, "Wow! That was close!" and so we give God a quick word of thanks for His angels. Even more pressing are those doctors' diagnoses that inform us of a chronic disease or something worse, something that might kill us at once.

So we cannot ignore death forever. At some point, it hits us, "I'm going to die"; and we confront the reality that if we live long enough, these bodies that we love so much—that we indulge and pamper and in which we parade and preen—these very bodies will let us down and we will die, each one of us personally. So how do we face that?

Just one way for Christians—make that two: by looking backward and by looking forward. We look back to Christ, who entered death before and for us. He is our example, for in spite of all that He suffered, when He finished His course, He died by committing His spirit to the Father (Luke 23:46). He is also our hope, for Jesus died precisely to rescue us from the fear of death: (Hebrews 2:14–15) "Since therefore the children share in flesh and blood, He Himself likewise partook of the same things, that through death He might destroy the one who has the power of death—that is, the devil—and deliver all those who through fear of death were subject to lifelong slavery."

Our Lord's death is our victory over our worst enemies. That's one reason we rejoice so much in our Baptism, for the Bible teaches that by Baptism God has incorporated us into the death of Christ. Paul used a rhetorical question to remind the Roman Christians of this: (Romans 6:3) "Do you not know that all of us who have been baptized into Christ Jesus were baptized into His death?" So, looking backward to our Baptism turns our gaze even further back to the death of Christ on our behalf as a victory over sin, death, and devil.

But our Lord did not remain dead. Jesus also came out of the tomb—alive—and His resurrection helps turn our gaze to the future, for the Scriptures call Him the "firstfruits of those who have fallen asleep" (1 Corinthians 15:20). He is the first of many, many people who will likewise arise from the dead. So we have God's promise that we too will come back from the grave at the end of time: (1 Corinthians 15:52–53) "The trumpet will sound, and the dead will be raised imperishable, and we shall be changed. For this perishable body must put on the imperishable, and this mortal body must put on immortality." This is God's Word, and that means that it is absolutely reliable. So even as our bodies are giving out now, we know that then they will arise again, but this time without sin or any of its consequences—absolutely incorruptible. That's the future to which we are looking, even when we are looking at death.

Conclusion

Clearly, therefore, what the Scriptures teach about the end of time is a source of endless inspiration and encouragement. On the one hand, thoughts of judgment encourage us to persist in faith and well-doing. Because of Christ's complete saving work, we are perfectly placed to remain Christians in heart and deed right up until the second coming. We know that the future is guaranteed by the love of Christ, so we can spend whatever time is left to us here in serving God by serving others, remaining faithful in whatever circumstances we find ourselves, even intense persecution.

On the other hand, God's promise of resurrection and an end to all evils is a mighty comfort and encouragement when we are experiencing them, including death—our own and that of loved ones. The second coming is no cause for fear or dread but rather provides every reason for hope and perseverance. Something good is going to happen—something very good!—and no one can take it away. After all, God has promised it.

Concluding Activities

Conclude the session with an appropriate prayer and announce the next *LifeLight* topic.

Small-Group Leaders Material

COVER: *Last Judgement* (detail), by Hans Memling. SuperStock/SuperStock

Last Things

Matthew 3:2, 11–12

Preparing for the Session

Central Focus

The main purpose of this lecture is to offer reasons for a study of the end times. Students will learn that the second coming of Jesus (along with the resurrection and judgment) are essential elements in the Christian religion—elements that offer great motivation for Christian living and great comfort in Christian dying. Students will also learn that the Bible has a great deal to say about the end times. This theme is a vital part of the Christian religion.

Objectives

That participants, led by the Holy Spirit working through God's Word, will

1. realize how important are God's promises about the last things;

2. learn that teachings about the last things are pervasive in the New Testament; and

3. prepare for the end in view of what God has revealed.

For the Small-Group Leader

Small-Group Discussion Helps

Day 1 • 2 Peter 3:4; 1 Corinthians 15:19; Revelation 7:16–17; 2 Peter 3:9; Matthew 24:14

1. Answers will vary but will certainly include sentiments such as "People don't care about the end" or "People don't believe the world will ever end." Of course, some people believe in the millennium and so treat the modern state of Israel as if it were a sign of the last days. Many worldly, nonreligious people are like Peter's scoffers, though.

2. Answers will vary, but one answer will certainly be that Christians would be pitied because all the promises of deliverance (from sins, death, and the devil) that they trusted in would be worthless if there is no life after this one.

3. God promises that there will be no more hunger or thirst, not too much heat, no more sorrow, springs of living water, and the presence of God, according to Revelation 7:16–17. Of course, students may bring up other promises as well, such as eternal life and a glorified body. People are more likely to think about these things at times when they are suffering from the lack of such things.

4. Christ hasn't returned yet because God is patient and desires that everyone should have a chance to repent and believe. The only real preparation is faith and everything that flows from faith.

5. Only the Church can evangelize the world. Therefore, the Church should do the work that Jesus gave her to do, especially to preach the Gospel to every creature (see Mark 16:15).

Day 2 • Matthew 3:2, 11–12; 1:23; 12:28; Luke 17:21; Matthew 25:1–13; 7:21–23

6. John the Baptist proclaimed that the time of judgment was at hand and that the coming Messiah would be the judge.

7. We can certainly say that the kingdom of heaven arrived when Jesus began His earthly ministry, because Jesus is the King! Relationship with Him determines one's place in the Kingdom.

8. The parable refers to the second coming of Jesus, for which we must be ready (i.e., faithful) right up until He arrives.

9. There will be some who are condemned in spite of their tremendous deeds. Although they may have done miracles, they did not obey the words of Jesus. Christ the Judge looks for faith that produces good works, not for miracles.

Day 3 • Mark 13:26–27; Luke 21:27–28; John 5:28–29; 11:24–25

10. In Mark's Gospel, we read that when Christ comes again in glory, He will send the angels to gather the elect from every part of the globe.

11. Luke adds that Christians should realize that their final redemption is drawing near.

12. In John, we also read that on the Last Day, Jesus will summon all people from their graves in order to pronounce a final judgment upon them.

13. (a) Jesus said that whoever believes in Him will receive the resurrection to life. (b) From this, we can clearly see that it is solely faith in Jesus that determines whether one rises to life or to judgment.

14. The Last Day brings with it the final blessings of Christ to all believers, including resurrection of the body. Without the Last Day, the Christian hope for eternal life and resurrection would be worthless and the Bible would be full of false promises.

Day 4 • Acts 10:42; 17:31; Romans 2:6–8; 2 Timothy 4:1–2; James 5:8; 2 Peter 3:10

15. Both Peter and Paul affirm that Jesus will be the world's final judge.

16. In Romans 2, Paul writes that God will judge everyone on the basis of his works. (Cf. Matthew 25:31–46.)

17. Jesus is described as being the judge of the living and the dead. In view of Christ's coming again, Timothy was supposed to "preach the Word . . . reprove, rebuke, and exhort."

18. (a) James informs us that, in light of the judgment to come, we are to be patient and "establish," that is, strengthen, our hearts. (b) Peter writes that on the Last Day, the heavens and the earth would be destroyed, and the final judgment would then take place.

19. Answers may vary but should include the realization that without Christ's return in glory, there would be no point to the Christian religion.

Day 5 • Acts 1:11; Matthew 28:20; 2 Thessalonians 3:11–13; Matthew 24:36; John 21:17; 1 Thessalonians 5:2

20. **Challenge question.** The angel promised that Jesus will come again from heaven as He went away into heaven. Even though Jesus ascended into heaven and we wait for His return to earth, Jesus is still present everywhere, since He is God and keeps His promises. So Jesus has gone from us and will return, but He remains with us always. Though these statements may seem to contradict, they actually do not. He is present with us now, but His presence now is invisible. We do not see it, but we believe it. However, at the end of time, everyone will see Him, whether they have been believers or not.

21. Paul urged the Thessalonians to wait for the Lord's coming by spending their time doing their work quietly and earning their own living.

22. Jesus knows everything according to His divine nature; but during His time on earth (i.e., His state of humiliation), He did not always and fully use His divine powers, including His divine omniscience. He grew hungry, became tired, and limited Himself in what He knew, including the time of His own second coming.

23. Paul describes Christ's second coming as being like the coming of a thief in the night. This image is used to depict how surprised people will be when He returns. Just as people know that they could conceivably be robbed someday but still never expect it when it happens, so also will Jesus' return be. People know that He could return at any time, but still they will be surprised the instant the end comes.

24. "Modern" Christians also need to be "biblical" ones; and the Bible teaches the second coming of Christ. Furthermore, "modern" Christians, just as much as Christians from earlier times, look forward to Christ's return, for then we will enjoy the fulfillment of all of God's promises to us, especially the resurrection of the body and life everlasting with Him.

Death and Dying

Romans 6:23

Preparing for the Session

Central Focus

Participants will be reminded that besides the end of the universe, everyone has an individual end, "death," for which we must all be ready. Many people want to think of death as "natural," just a part of the way things are in a material universe. But that is not so. Death is the result of sin. Our Lord Jesus Christ has overcome sin and death so that believers can face the end of life with confidence.

Objectives

That participants, led by the Holy Spirit working through God's Word, will

1. realize that death is not a natural conclusion to human life but God's punishment for sin;

2. learn that Christ's death and resurrection are God's answer to sin and death; and

3. on account of God's love in Christ, live in expectation of eternal life and resurrection when they die.

For the Small-Group Leader

Small-Group Discussion Helps

Day 1 • "Thanatopsis" (selections); Genesis 3:19; Isaiah 40:6–7

1. The underlying thought of the poem is that death is purely natural; it is something that happens to everybody and so everybody should just accept it. Don't worry about it. You can't stop it anyway. Certainly, a lot of people seem to think this way: that when you're dead, you're dead; that is all there is. People like this will believe that there is no heaven or hell, no afterlife at all.

2. Death is a result of sin, beginning with Adam. It happens to all of us because we all are sinners.

3. Answers will vary, but one of the ways is certainly our efforts at "dressing up" death to make it appear as if a person were simply sleeping.

4. *For personal reflection. Sharing optional.* Human death is likened with the death of grass. Grass grows for a while and thrives, but then it withers and dies.

5. (a) God is the one who is in charge of life and death, although we may at various times and in various ways act as though we are. (b) Whether this is good news depends on one's relationship with God, but it certainly is important. Too many people ignore this reality and so endanger themselves for eternity.

Day 2 • Read Genesis 2:17; Ezekiel 18:20, 32; Genesis 8:21; Romans 8:7–8; Ecclesiastes 7:2; Romans 7:19–20

6. We die because we are fallen and sinful. Death is the punishment for sin. Since all sin, all deserve to die. In fact, we are even born in a sinful condition; see Psalm 51:5.

7. The Bible is very clear that all people sin. For as long as this present world stands, we will all face death, demonstrating that we are all sinful. In fact, no matter how hard we may try to stop sinning and live lives pleasing to God, we will continue sinning all throughout our lives. This is demonstrated especially in Romans 7:19–20.

8. We are sinful right from conception and birth. We inherit sinfulness from our parents, going all the way back to Adam. We call this "original sin." That is the tragedy of the human condition. We are not forced to sin. We do so willingly. So often, we eagerly want to sin.

9. Yes. Coming to faith in Christ does not prevent us from sinning; unfortunately, we remain sinners. Remember that Jesus instructed His disciples always to pray for forgiveness in the Lord's Prayer: "and forgive us our trespasses as we forgive those who trespass against us." We experience an ongoing battle between our old sinful nature and the "new man" that desires to serve God in righteousness and holiness. This tension continues in us all our lives. Our sinful nature will remain a part of us until we lay it down in death. Then all that will remain will be the new creature that we are in Christ.

10. God sent His Son, Jesus, into the world to be our Savior and to deliver us from the guilt and eternal consequences of our sins.

Day 3 • Romans 5:8; Acts 17:32; Matthew 28:11–15; Acts 8:1–3

11. God loved us when we were still unrepentant sinners. In other words, He loved us first. Christ died for us, and the Bible tells us many times about God's unconditional love for us in Christ.

12. (a) The intellectuals did not react favorably to the message of the resurrection of the body. Some of them mocked Paul, and others just put him off. (b) People have continued to react in these ways to the Gospel promise of the resurrection. The Christian religion is mocked by many so-called intellectuals and even professional comedians. Many others just ignore Christ altogether.

13. The Jewish leaders responded to the message of the resurrection of Jesus by bribing the guards to lie and say that the disciples had stolen the body, even though this was extremely unlikely.

14. (a) Answers may vary. However, it should be noted that people are often threatened by the Gospel because it requires repentance and faith. That means admitting when one has done wrong and making a change in one's "lifestyle." (b) Some people find the idea of "hell" more threatening than the denial of an afterlife altogether. Better nothing at all than punishment.

15. If Jesus really is the Son of God, then we need to listen to His Word and follow what He says. That means faithfulness in the face of mockery or persecution or death—just like Paul, Peter, and Christians in every age. But it also means living—and dying—in a certain hope of everlasting life and bodily resurrection.

Day 4 • 1 John 1:1–3; Acts 1:22; 1 Corinthians 15:5–8; Acts 8:1–3

16. There were witnesses. In the Scriptures, we read that ordinary people—like you and me—saw Him dead and risen again.

17. There were many witnesses. There were even more than five hundred of them at one time. They likely included Peter, Paul, the other disciples, Mary Magdalene and the other women at the empty tomb, and John, as well as many others. They were people like most Christians today—not the elites or powerful.

18. (a) Later on, many of these witnesses were persecuted or even martyred. (b) They endured those trials because they persisted in telling others about the resurrected Christ, even though some of those "others" didn't want to listen. Some of those other people so hated the Gospel of salvation that they attempted to prevent its spread and to destroy the Church.

19. Answers will vary. For some people, it means nothing at all and they're just not interested in hearing about it. For others, it is only a story symbolizing the coming of spring, hope, and new life. For others, it is old-fashioned, superstitious nonsense. But most important, we know the accounts of Christ's resurrection to be historically true and the foundation for the Christian religion.

20. *For personal reflection. Sharing optional.* Answers will vary.

Day 5 • "Death Be Not Proud" by John Donne; Isaiah 40:8

21. People are likely to feel this way about death if they think of it as being either the absolute end with no afterlife following it or if they see it as being the entrance into an unknown eternity. The people who are most likely to think in these ways would certainly include atheists, agnostics, and modernists of every sort. Also, believers in non-Christian religions who think that they determine their own fate on the basis of their works would likely also be fearful about death. They would regard death as bringing a judgment on how well they had actually done in life.

22. "Rest of their bones, and soul's delivery." Their souls are delivered from condemnation and taken to be with Christ, while their mortal remains are laid to rest in the earth.

23. The poet writes that "One short sleep past, we wake eternally." He refers to the resurrection of the body at the end of time. Not only will our souls be delivered from death but our bodies will be as well. On the Last Day, the dead indeed will rise. God will abolish death forever!

24. (a) Isaiah proclaims that "the word of our God" lasts forever. (b) That's precisely what we are relying on, and since it is God's Word, we can rely on it absolutely in every situation, even death.

Heaven or Hell

Matthew 10:28; Luke 23:46

Preparing for the Session

Central Focus

When a person dies, his soul goes to heaven or hell. All of us deserve hell on account of our sins, but Christ has opened paradise to believers.

Objectives

That participants, led by the Holy Spirit working through God's Word, will

1. understand that a person consists of body and soul;

2. learn that when a Christian dies, his soul goes to heaven; and

3. appreciate that heaven is purely a gift that God offers to sinners for the sake of Jesus.

For the Small-Group Leader

Small-Group Discussion Helps

Day 1 • Genesis 2:7; Matthew 10:28; 26:38; Luke 23:46, 53–55; 1 Peter 3:19–20; 1 Thessalonians 5:23; Mark 12:30

1. (a) Allow people to share their thoughts. (b) Answers will vary, but the leader needs to make the point that certainty about what happens at the time of death rests with the Bible because it is God's Word.

2. Genesis 2:7 describes humans as made from the "dust from the ground" and "the breath of life." The two principal parts of a human being are body and soul.

3. Matthew 10:28 says, "Fear Him who can destroy both soul and body in hell"; that is, fear God. Here we also see that man is comprised of a body and a soul.

4. (a) Jesus prayed, "Father, into Your hands I commit My spirit!" (Luke 23:46). His soul was going to heaven to be with the Father. (b) After He was again brought to life, He descended into hell. During His descent into hell, we read that Jesus preached to "the spirits in prison"; that is, the souls of the dead in hell, especially those who were disobedient at the time of Noah.

5. **Challenge question.** The number of aspects that make up a human being remains an "open question" as to whether the Scriptures teach a twofold nature of man (body and soul) or a threefold (body, soul, and spirit), or more, since Jesus lists four aspects in Mark 12:30 (heart, soul, mind, and strength). Trying to get a definitive list or count seems beside the point, since human beings are certainly complicated! Perhaps it is simpler to say that mankind is body (material) and soul (immaterial). The reference in 1 Thessalonians to "spirit" could mean the religious nature of a believer. In other words, it could refer to the new man that we become when baptized.

Day 2 • Genesis 3:19; Ecclesiastes 12:7; 1 Corinthians 15:54–55; 1:7–8; Philippians 3:20–21; 1:19–26

6. (a) At death, the body decays. This means that its constituent elements dissipate and become parts of other natural things, such as the atmosphere, worms, or earth. (b) Meanwhile, at death, the soul goes to either heaven or hell.

7. Death is conquered and victory will be fully enjoyed with the resurrection of the body at the end of time.

8. We are waiting for the physical return of our Lord on the Last Day and the transformation of our bodies into a glorified state.

9. (a) Paul saw only two possible ends to his imprisonment. Either he would be freed and continue his ministry or he would be executed. (b) Paul's preference was to pass through death. He writes that "to die is gain" and "to depart and be with Christ, for that is far better."

10. Christians can know for sure that their soul will be with God in an ongoing and blissful relationship.

Day 3 • Luke 23:46; Galatians 4:4–6; Luke 23:43; Genesis 2:8, 10; Revelation 14:13; Acts 7:55–60

11. Immediately before His death, Jesus called God "Father." He committed His spirit (soul) to God.

12. (a) Jesus calls on us to address God as "Abba," that is, "Father." He encourages us to call God by the personal and intimate term for one's own father. This is possible because we have been baptized into Christ and we believe His promises. Therefore, we are God's adopted sons and He is our Father. (b) This is significant for us because it means that at the time of our own death, we, too, can commend our souls to God, knowing that He will deliver us through death to the blessedness beyond.

13. Jesus promised that the penitent thief would be with Him in paradise. The use of this term demonstrates to us that the place that our souls will be taken to has neither sin nor the consequences of sin. There will be no pain, loss, temptation, or any other evil.

14. The passage in Revelation describes these people as being "blessed." Also, "they may rest from their labors." All the things—including our own sinful nature—that cause this life to be anything but blessed will be gone. That's good—very good. No wonder that Paul thought of dying in Christ as "far better" than earthly life.

15. (a) Immediately before his death, Stephen saw a vision of heaven, with Jesus on the right hand of the Father. This suggests that the soul enjoys a beatific vision of the ascended Lord. (b) Regardless of our earthly circumstances, we know that our death is simply the entranceway for our soul into a far better existence in heaven in the visible presence of God.

Day 4 • Luke 23:39–43; Matthew 5:21–22; Romans 3:23; John 3:16; 11:25–27

16. Certainly, heaven is not for those who deserve it, for none of us ever could be so deserving. Here with the penitent thief, we see that heaven is open to those who put their trust in Jesus. We cannot claim that we have, even to the smallest degree, been good enough to merit heaven. We can consider that the thief was a criminal being executed—justly, he admits—for his crimes. It is never a matter of people being good enough or not good enough for heaven. It is entirely a matter of faith in Christ.

17. (a) Whoever is angry with his brother or calls him a fool has broken the Fifth Commandment and deserves punishment. (b) The commandments forbid not just overt acts but also everything that could lead up to those acts, including evil thoughts and words.

18. *For personal reflection. Sharing optional.* No one deserves to go to heaven when they die. We are all sinful, so we all deserve to be condemned forever to hell. Heaven is a gracious gift from our Lord.

19. (a) The promise of eternal life is grounded in God's love for sinful humanity, as demonstrated by the saving work of Jesus. This gift from God is received simply by believing in Him—that is, putting one's trust in God's promises of eternal life and forgiveness on account of Jesus' saving work. (b) No. Christ has fulfilled all righteousness and done all things for us.

20. Whoever believes in Jesus and dies will live again. Whoever is alive and believes in Jesus will never die. God is in charge of death and resurrection. We cannot control either one. We may simply rely on Him for the gift of the resurrection of the body and life everlasting, which He gives us through our faith in Christ.

Day 5 • 1 Peter 3:19–20; Matthew 8:12; 25:41; Luke 16:23–24; John 3:17–18; Genesis 3:15

21. Those who refuse to trust in the righteousness of Christ are condemned by their sins. They go to hell.

22. Without hell, God's justice would be incomplete. There really would be no real reason for being good instead of evil. Both would be the same if the result of each was also the same. So many people today are materialists; that is, they don't believe in any spiritual or supernatural reality. Other people don't want to admit there is a hell, since they don't want to go there. Most don't want to admit they are sinners, let alone people who deserve eternal punishment.

23. Hell is described in a variety of ways, including "prison," "outer darkness," "weeping and gnashing of teeth," "eternal fire," "torment," and "flame."

24. Through the salvation God provides for us in Jesus, we see that He is merciful. Forgiveness is available to all because Jesus died for all.

25. Answers will vary. But the main thing is that there is forgiveness for every sin, including the worst that one can think of, in the saving work of Jesus—His perfect life in our stead; His suffering and death on the cross, which paid the punishment for sin; and His resurrection, which demonstrated His complete victory over sin, death, and hell. All of that is ours simply through faith in Him.

Judgment in the Old Testament

Psalm 96:12–13

Preparing for the Session

Central Focus

We can see that from the first days of human history, God has punished wickedness. This is a theme that permeates the Old Testament, but judgment is also associated with the coming of the Messiah. That same figure is portrayed as the Redeemer through whom God will show mercy to the penitent.

Objectives

That participants, led by the Holy Spirit working through God's Word, will

1. realize that God's punishment of the wicked is a principal theme of the Old Testament;

2. understand that God also offers mercy and forgiveness in the Old Testament; and

3. learn that God's Word will prepare them for the judgment that will culminate in the coming of the Messiah.

For the Small-Group Leader

Small-Group Discussion Helps

Day 1 • Psalm 96:12–13; Amos 9:8–10; Genesis 3:16–19; Romans 5:12; Psalm 50

1. The Lord is coming to judge the earth. He will judge the world in righteousness and the peoples in His faithfulness. This is a good thing, because God will make all things right instead of letting the world continue on in evil, which seems always to grow stronger.

2. The threats in this portion of Amos were leveled at "the house of Jacob" and "the house of Israel." These are both references to the chosen people, the Israelites, to whom God had shown His goodness and favor. God was threatening to judge them because of their sins.

3. (a) Since the fall, God sends punishment on everyone. The sin of Adam and Eve resulted in a punishment upon them and all their descendants. The result of this has been hard, laborious work and pain in childbirth. All people are also under the curse of death. (b) Who are we to ask whether God is "fair"? But in point of fact, Paul points out that all people have continued in sin, like their ancestor Adam.

4. God judges the "faithful," that is, those who have followed the Old Testament sacrificial system, and the wicked among Israel. The first group obeys the Law outwardly but does not give God thanks, keep vows, or call upon God in trouble. The second group disobeys God outwardly—taking pleasure in thieves and adulterers, lying and slandering.

5. **Challenge question.** Christianity is more than outward activities such as attending church. God wants piety in the heart—faith, repentance, and the fruits thereof. It is also true that many so-called Christians show that Christianity means nothing to them, because they live just like unbelievers. And yet, in those same outward activities, God sees the heart. Through the old covenant sacrifices, He offered genuine forgiveness, just as He does now in the Word and Sacrament ministry of the church today. In the sacrifices of the Old Testament, He pointed forward to the all-availing sacrifice of Jesus for sinners.

Day 2 • Genesis 19:4–5, 24–25; 1 Kings 11:9–13; 2 Kings 17:6–12; 23:27; 21:1–9; 25:20–21

6. The cities were totally destroyed by fire and sulfur from heaven. The specific sin mentioned is homosexual rape. The word *know* is used in the sense of sexual intercourse. *Sodomy* gets its name from Sodom.

7. (a) Solomon's kingdom was split into two parts after Solomon's death. God separated the northern ten tribes of Israel from being ruled by Solomon's descendants. Solomon's sin was that of worshiping other gods. (b) God reserved one tribe and the city of Jerusalem to Solomon's descendants on account of His promise to David.

8. **Challenge question.** God will not put up forever with those who defile His name and worship false gods. There are still many false religions in the world, and some, like Islam, are growing here in the United States.

Many people commit "fine idolatry"; that is, instead of the true God, they make money, fame, or pleasure the most important things in their lives.

9. God is always the same. That means He will punish such sins eventually. Yet, even as He was gracious to the descendants of David, He is ever ready to forgive on account of Jesus, the Son of David.

Day 3 • Genesis 6:5–7; 7:21–23; Matthew 24:37–39

10. God saw that man's wickedness was great all over the earth. Every intention of man's thoughts was evil.

11. The destruction caused by the flood was complete. All flesh died—animals, birds, insects, and human beings. It was appropriate because people used the world and its resources for their own evil purposes.

12. Noah, his family, and all the animals in the ark were spared. This shows us that in the midst of His righteous judgment, God was merciful.

13. (a) Life went on as usual—people were even getting married right up until the time the flood started. (b) They completely ignored the signs of coming judgment. After all, Noah was building an ark and preparing for judgment for perhaps as long as one hundred years (compare Genesis 5:32 and 7:6) before it finally came.

14. **Challenge question.** People will be just the same: living as if the earth—with all its wickedness—was going to last forever and ignoring the signs of the coming judgment. It seems evident that many (perhaps even most) people are completely indifferent to moral wickedness and are living as if everything is going to stay just the same. Yet, God generously provides for salvation in the gift of His Son and His life-giving Word.

Day 4 • Genesis 7:1–5; 19:29; 2 Chronicles 36:22–23; Judges 2:11, 14, 18; Jonah 1:2; 3:10; 4:1–2; Jeremiah 31:31–34

15. Neither Noah nor Lot deserved to be rescued—absolutely not. For example, after the flood, Noah became completely drunk (Genesis 9:20–27), as did Lot after he was delivered from Sodom; Lot also committed incest (Genesis 19:30–38).

16. When the time of the Babylonian captivity was complete, God showed mercy on His people and brought them out of captivity and restored them to Judea and Jerusalem.

17. These events reveal God's undeserved mercy toward sinners. In Judges, we see a continual pattern of the people sinning and being punished, then repenting, and God sending a rescuer when they did not deserve one at all.

18. (a) Clearly the people of Nineveh deserved to be punished by God. They were a wicked and idolatrous people. (b) Nevertheless, the city was spared. God did not destroy the city after the people in it repented. He had mercy on it, especially on account of the little children and the animals. Jonah was angry that God did not destroy Nineveh.

19. (a) The first covenant was a mutual relationship established by God at the time of the exodus. It was based on the Law, but the people broke it. (b) The new covenant would be based on the forgiveness of sins.

Day 5 • Genesis 3:14–19; Isaiah 11:1–9; Daniel 7:13–14; Mark 14:62

20. (a) The serpent's punishment was that it would from then on have to crawl around on its belly. (b) Eve's punishment was pain in childbirth and being placed under the rule of her husband. (c) Adam's punishment was that his life would consist of hard work, resulting from God's cursing the ground.

21. Yes. In talking to the serpent, God promised an offspring of the woman who would bruise the serpent's head, even though the serpent would bruise His heel. This promise was fulfilled in Jesus. He took on our flesh and blood and was born of Mary. Through His perfect, innocent life, sacrificial death, and resurrection, He achieved for us the forgiveness of sins and defeated the devil, the one who had worked through the serpent in the garden. Although on the cross Christ was hurt (depicted in the promise as His heel being bruised by the snake), He triumphed over the enemy and defeated him (depicted as the serpent's head being crushed).

22. Isaiah describes the promised Messiah as being a descendant of Jesse (the father of David). (a) The Spirit of the Lord would be upon Him. He would delight in God. (b) He would judge the world with complete fairness by His Word. (c) He would establish a world of perfect peace and harmony.

23. Daniel is given a vision of the coming of Christ. Specifically, Daniel is shown someone arriving on the clouds, like "a son of man." God gives this Son of Man a kingdom of glory. All people would serve Him, and His kingdom would last forever.

24. **Challenge question.** Through His suffering and death, our Lord overcame the devil, death, and sin (and all its consequences). Now we live by the forgiveness of sins and the promises of eternal life and resurrection. Jesus will return again in glory to accomplish all of His promises and establish a new heaven and a new earth in which sin and evil will be gone forever.

Judgment Day
Matthew 25:31–46

Preparing for the Session

Central Focus

Judgment Day is an essential aspect of the work of Jesus. John the Baptist prophesied it, and Jesus Himself promised it and described it. In order to be ready for Judgment Day, the basic requirement is faith. But true faith is always active in love toward one's neighbor. That will be evident to all on the Last Day.

Objectives

That participants, led by the Holy Spirit working through God's Word, will

1. realize that judging the living and dead at the end of time is an essential aspect of the work of Jesus;

2. understand that the only real preparation for Judgment Day is repentance and faith; and

3. exercise true faith active in love.

For the Small-Group Leader

Small-Group Discussion Helps

Day 1 • Malachi 4; Matthew 11:13–14; 3:1–2; Mark 1:4–5; Luke 3:8–14; Matthew 3:10

1. Malachi describes the Day of the Lord as a burning fire that will consume the wicked while the Lord's people tread them underfoot. God promised to send Elijah as a forerunner of His coming.

2. Jesus tells us that this prophecy was fulfilled in John the Baptist. John's message of judgment was similar to Elijah's. John's bravery in rebuking even kings like Herod the Tetrarch (see Matthew 14:3–4) was also reminiscent of Elijah (see 1 Kings 17:1).

3. Matthew records the content of John's preaching as "Repent, for the kingdom of heaven is at hand." Jesus also came proclaiming this message of repentance and the coming of the kingdom of heaven.

4. *For personal reflection. Sharing optional.* The sincerity of one's repentance is demonstrated by the fruits of repentance; that is, replacing one's sinful works by good works that flow from faith. The Lord teaches us to do such works not to impress others but to do so before Him (e.g., Matthew 6:1–6, 16–21). In contrast, church leaders have at times urged or required repentant persons to make public displays of their works, such as the early medieval system of public penance, the late medieval rule that penitent people had to enumerate all of their sins in confession, and Protestant groups who taught their members to prove their election to eternal life through public acts. Such practices have commonly led to grave abuses.

5. John the Baptist was preaching specifically about God's kingdom coming in judgment. John and Malachi were both pointing forward to the coming of the Lord to render a final judgment upon mankind, including a final punishment of the wicked.

Day 2 • Matthew 3:11–12; Luke 24:44; John 5:39; Matthew 11:2–6

6. (a) The Messiah's twofold work would involve making a final judgment upon humanity by taking the faithful into His kingdom and by punishing the wicked. (b) John compares this to the process of threshing grain, which separates the good part from the chaff.

7. Everything in the Old Testament about Him had to be fulfilled. He pointed His opponents to the Scriptures. This demonstrates to us that the Old Testament—like the New—is entirely about Jesus Christ. He is promised in the Old Testament; and in the New Testament, we read about the fulfillment of that promise.

8. Jesus referred John's disciples to His miracles of healing and resurrection and to His preaching the Gospel to the poor. These were works of the Messiah, promised in the Old Testament. Even though Jesus had not yet ushered in the final judgment, clearly His works demonstrated that He is the Christ.

9. The Church continues Jesus' work of showing mercy toward the suffering and of evangelizing poor sinners. He especially wants to give people an opportunity to repent and believe.

Day 3 • John 5:27; Acts 10:42; 2 Corinthians 5:10; 2 Timothy 4:1; Revelation 22:12, 20

10. Jesus said that on that day He would execute judgment. The Father has given Him this task.

11. Jesus is the one whom God has appointed to be the judge of the living and of the dead.

12. (a) Paul reminds the Corinthians of the coming of Judgment Day. (b) When charging Timothy to preach the Word, Paul did so in the presence of God and Christ Jesus, who is going to judge the living and the dead.

13. (a) Jesus said He would be coming soon to repay everyone for what each has done. (b) John did not respond with fear or dread. Rather, his response was a prayer that the Lord indeed would come.

14. (a) As we consistently see from the answers to the above questions, and as we can read all throughout the Scriptures, Christ's specific purpose in coming on the Last Day is to judge the living and the dead. (b) Answers will vary; however, like John, we do not need to dread or fear the day of the Lord's coming. Trusting in the grace of God in Jesus, we will stand in the judgment and be welcomed by Christ into eternity. "Amen. Come, Lord Jesus!"

Day 4 • Matthew 5:3–12; 7:21–23; 11:21–24; 12:36–37; 16:26–27; 18:8–9; 26:64

15. (a) The blessing of the first (Matthew 5:3) and eighth (v. 10) beatitudes is the same: "the kingdom of heaven." The blessings of the second through seventh are in the future (rather than the present) tense. (b) In the last part of the Sermon on the Mount, Jesus makes it clear that one gets into the kingdom of heaven only by doing the will of God—not by using the Lord's name, not even by doing marvelous works.

16. (a) Their condemnation would be worse than those cities renowned for their wickedness. (b) They had ignored the mighty works done in their midst by Jesus and had rejected what those works indicated about Jesus.

17. (a) The judgment will be extremely thorough. It would include even words spoken carelessly. (b) Answers will vary. But the point of the Law is to convict us of sin.

18. *For personal reflection. Sharing optional.* These are rhetorical questions. None of the things that we sinfully value in this life is worth the cost of our lives. Realize that the human situation is still fundamentally the same in the light of God's coming judgment. It is the height of foolishness to prefer the passing temptations of this life to an eternal life with God.

19. (a) Our sin comes from the heart. This does not refer to the physical organ, of course, but rather to the inner self—the sinful human nature we are born with. (b) The only real way to prepare is repentance and faith in the Savior.

Day 5 • Matthew 25:31–46; Daniel 7:13–14; Matthew 1:21; 20:28; Romans 3:28; James 2:16–17

20. (a) Judgment Day will come when Jesus arrives in His glory, sits upon His throne, and gathers all people before Him. The people will at once be separated into two groups: "the sheep and the goats." (b) Jesus Christ—who knows all our thoughts and words—is not interrogating anyone so that He can make a judgment. Instead, He is publicly providing a rationale for the judgment He has already made.

21. Jesus would save His people from their sins. The name Jesus means "the Lord saves."

22. (a) Jesus accomplished this by giving His life as a ransom; that is, by taking our place and our obligations under God's Law, by suffering and dying for our sins. (b) We are saved through faith alone; that is, by trusting God's Word, which tells us that by the work of Jesus we are perfectly reconciled with God.

23. Works are the way we show our gratitude to God for His mercy in Christ. They are the fruit of faith but add nothing to it for our salvation. They simply demonstrate that we are what we say we are, namely, believers in Jesus.

24. Works are necessary. Every Christian must (and wants) to do them. But works are not necessary for salvation, because Christ has done it all.

Resurrection

1 Corinthians 15:35–49

Preparing for the Session

Central Focus

This lesson emphasizes two things: (1) the importance of the resurrection of the body for the Gospel, which is a doctrine of immense comfort—without it, Christianity is no longer Christianity; and (2) the biblical basis for this doctrine in both the Old and New Testaments.

Objectives

That participants, led by the Holy Spirit working through God's Word, will

1. understand the biblical basis for the doctrine of the resurrection;

2. realize that since our Lord's resurrection came first, ours shall surely follow at the end of time; and

3. appreciate the hope and comfort that the resurrection of the body offers believers in the face of death—that of loved ones and also their own.

For the Small-Group Leader

Small-Group Discussion Helps

Day 1 • 1 Corinthians 15:12–19; Luke 20:37–38; Isaiah 26:19; Daniel 12:2; Job 19:25–27

1. If there is no resurrection from the dead, then Christ has not been raised. If Christ has not been raised, the Christian faith is futile and we are still in our sins. If Christ is still in the tomb, then death and the devil won the battle, not Jesus. That means that His suffering and death did not free us from anything, especially our sins, because death—the winner—is the punishment for sin.

2. Jesus answered the Sadducees by referring them to God's self-description: "the God of Abraham and the God of Isaac and the God of Jacob." From our perspective, these men are long dead, but not from God's, since all live to Him. It wouldn't make sense to believe in an almighty Creator of the universe who cannot bring people back from the dead. See also Luke 1:37.

3. (a) Isaiah stated that "Your dead shall live; their bodies shall rise." (b) Daniel describes a twofold resurrection: "some to everlasting life, and some to shame and everlasting contempt."

4. His words are very confident: "I know." He talks about seeing God in his flesh and with his own eyes.

5. (a) Answers will vary. One important point to make is about the philosophical materialism of our times. People think that "stuff"—that which we experience with our senses in this life—is the only reality. They also believe that the universe is limited to natural laws and processes. They accept a "scientific" worldview that has no room for the spiritual or the supernatural. Besides, if God is real and the Scriptures are true, such people will have to change how they live! (b) No. That is Paul's point in 1 Corinthians 15:17.

Day 2 • Matthew 25:32, 46; 2 Corinthians 5:10; John 5:25–29; 6:40

6. In that text, we read that all the nations will be there. "We must all appear" before Christ in judgment.

7. (a) The Father has given to His Son the task of judgment, so the Son will summon all from their graves to receive their final sentence. (b) Some will come forth to the "resurrection of life" and others to the "resurrection of judgment."

8. "Everyone who looks on the Son and believes in Him."

9. Life was created by God. Note that this creative work was performed not just by the Father but also by the Son (see John 1:3) and the Holy Spirit (see Genesis 1:2). Raising the dead is no obstacle to the Creator.

Day 3 • Acts 24:14–15; 2 Corinthians 5:10; Romans 2:5–11; 3:20, 23–24; Matthew 25:34

10. Paul stated that he believed everything God had given us in the Old Testament. Specifically, he believed that there will be a resurrection of the just and unjust.

11. Everyone will receive what he is due on the basis of what he has done while alive, whether good or evil.

12. (a) He will use the standard of what people have done, their works—those who have been patient in well-doing and those who have been self-seeking and obedient to unrighteousness. (b) Everybody will be held to this same standard.

13. On account of God's mercy, He has sent His Son, Jesus, to be humanity's substitute and to pay the penalty under the Law. Therefore, when people trust in Him, God places Christ's righteousness on them and declares them not guilty in His sight.

Day 4 • John 11:23–25, 43–44; Luke 7:14–15; 8:54–55; John 20:27; Luke 24:39, 42; Romans 6:9–10; Matthew 25:31

14. (a) Lazarus was in the grave, dead for four days. (b) Jesus told Lazarus to come out, and he rose from the dead and came out of the tomb. (c) Likewise, on the Last Day, Jesus will summon all the dead from their graves.

15. The young man of Nain, Jairus's daughter, and nameless others arose only to die again. Our resurrections at the end of time will be permanent and will result in glorified bodies.

16. Jesus invited them to touch Him; He ate some fish; they saw His wounds (hand, feet, and side). The Word of Life, who was from the beginning, was with the Father.

17. He had a glorified body, no longer subject to human frailties, which are the result of sin.

18. (a) Answers will vary. It's important to note that Jesus' resurrection was a real resurrection. The same person who had been dead was now alive—it was no trick or deception. That is also God's promise to us. (b) Answers will vary, but we should note that we, too, are looking forward to a final triumph over sin and its consequences in our lives. That is God's promise now, but we long for its fulfillment.

Day 5 • Philippians 3:20–21; 1 Corinthians 15:3–8, 20–23

19. Christ will change our bodies so that they will be like His glorified body.

20. Paul made a straightforward appeal to eyewitness testimony. He told skeptics about those who had seen Jesus after His resurrection. Although the witnesses are all dead, their testimony survives in the New Testament documents and in the story of their lives—their willingness to suffer all, including death, rather than deny their Lord.

21. (a) Jesus arose from the dead first, but all believers will arise from the dead in the same way at the end of time. Jesus is only the first. All believers will follow. (b) Death is not permanent. Bodies may lie lifeless in the ground now, but on the Last Day, they will come forth again just as if they were waking from sleep.

22. (a) Each person did something that affected all other people. (b) By Adam came sin and death to all humanity. By Jesus came the resurrection of the dead. (c) Answers will vary, but the difference seems more important. Death is the just penalty for our sins too; but resurrection is God's pure gift for Jesus' sake.

23. That promise would be futile, empty, and a terrible deception.

The Last Day

Matthew 24:29–31

Preparing for the Session

Central Focus

The purpose of this lesson is to study the Bible for what it says about the very end of time, the Last Day. Students will learn not only what all humanity can expect at the end but also that for believers it will be a Day of Triumph. The Last Day is really a part of the Gospel.

Objectives

That participants, led by the Holy Spirit working through God's Word, will

1. learn about the events of Judgment Day;

2. appreciate that readiness for the end consists of faith in Jesus, not only the world's judge but also our Savior; and

3. find encouragement and hope in the promise of a glorified body.

For the Small-Group Leader

Small-Group Discussion Helps

Day 1 • Matthew 24:29–31; 13:41–42; Luke 11:29–32; John 5:27–29; 6:40

1. (a) As the heavens collapse, Jesus will appear in the sky in power and glory. Humanity will mourn, but Christ will send out His angels to sound a trumpet and gather all the elect from every part of the globe. (b) These are the believers whom God has loved in Christ from all eternity and has sustained in the faith until the very end.

2. The angels sound the trumpet and gather the elect. But they will also cast the law-breakers out of Christ's kingdom and into hell.

3. Everyone will be there—even those long dead, like the Queen of Sheba (the South) who visited Solomon and like the men of Nineveh to whom Jonah preached.

4. The bodily resurrection of the dead will also take place on the Last Day.

5. Jesus is our Savior, the one in whom we will be saved when we believe in Him, just as God has promised.

Day 2 • Acts 1:11; 3:21; 24:15, 21; 23:6–8; 4:1–3; 17:31–32

6. An essential part of the disciples' message would be that Jesus would come again in the same way that they had seen Him go.

7. (a) "Until the time for restoring all the things about which God spoke by . . . His holy prophets" (Acts 3:21). (b) Peter believed that the second coming was definitely going to happen and would include the restoration of the world from sin and all its consequences; that is, the re-creation of a universe without wickedness.

8. Paul believed that there would be a resurrection of the just and of the unjust. What got Paul into trouble was his proclamation of Jesus being dead and risen again. This meant that Jesus was going to come again in order to judge the living and the dead and to end the rule of sin. People did not want to hear that.

9. (a) The Jewish leaders rejected Peter's message and persecuted the preachers (Peter and John). (b) Some made fun of Paul for his preaching, and others just dismissed him.

10. A final resurrection is connected to a final judgment. That means people need to change their ways. However, Christians should not change their doctrine. The truth is what saves. Changing or ignoring it will help nobody.

Day 3 • 2 Peter 3:12–13; Romans 2:6–10, 15–16; 1 Thessalonians 4:13–18; Romans 3:20, 24–25

11. People have used the things of the universe to carry out sin. Just think, for example, of how people have made false gods out of the sun, moon, and stars; trees and springs; and wood and rock carvings. They have used anything and everything as a replacement for the true God.

12. Paul told of tribulation and distress for evildoers, but glory, honor, and peace for those who do good.

13. (a) The dead in Christ will rise first to meet Christ as He descends to earth, then the believers who are still alive. (b) The faithful dead will arise from their graves. All believers shall remain always with the Lord.

14. (a) God provided another way to salvation besides the Law. He provided salvation through faith in Jesus Christ. "A propitiation" is a meritorious sacrifice or payment that satisfies God's anger against sin. (b) Answers will vary, but many will say things like "Jesus is the payment for my sin." Or, "Jesus satisfies God's anger against my sin." The Gospel is personal as well as universal.

15. Christ suffered and died to satisfy God's righteous anger against sin. That is God's justice. But Christ, the innocent Son of God, suffered and died instead of us who deserved the punishment. That is God's mercy.

Day 4 • 1 Corinthians 15:35–57; Luke 24:39–40; John 20:20, 24–29; 2 Corinthians 5:17

16. (a) A believer's body is placed into the ground just like a seed of grain is planted in the ground. From the latter comes the full-grown plant; from the former comes the glorified body. (b) Our earthly body tells us very little about our resurrected body, since the differences between them are so vast. Even so, the one comes from the other.

17. (a) "Perishable" and "imperishable"—the glorified body is no longer subject to death. (b) "Dishonor" and "glory"—the glorified body is no longer degraded by age and illness or decaying in the tomb but is now permanently in the way God intended and made it. (c) "Weakness" and "power"—the glorified body is no longer subject to whatever anybody wants to do with a corpse. (d) "Natural" and "spiritual"—the glorified body is no longer subject to all the consequences of Adam's sin but is now like the body of Christ, the conqueror of sin.

18. The one refers to unredeemed human beings, inheritors of sin and death from Adam. The second refers to likeness to Christ, alive forever in righteousness and purity.

19. (a) Jesus' body was the same. People could still see where He had been wounded on the cross. (b) All sin and the consequences thereof will be missing. There will be no more weaknesses, either physical or moral.

20. (a) It is true as a guaranteed promise from God. It gives us sure hope for the future. But we do not yet see it or experience it. (b) We will experience the "newness" perfectly.

Day 5 • Matthew 5:18; Luke 21:33; Matthew 24:29, 35; 2 Peter 3:5–13; 1 John 3:2

21. (a) Christ's Word will last forever. It is the basis for our eternal salvation. (b) On the Last Day, heaven and earth will pass away.

22. The universe will all be changed. Specifically, we read that the sun and moon will fall dark, and the stars will fall from heaven.

23. (a) Peter compared the final judgment coming on the Last Day with the judgment and destruction that fell upon the world during the great flood in the days of Noah. However, unlike the flood, the final destruction of the fallen world will be by fire rather than by water. (b) This will usher in the new heavens and a new earth—"in which righteousness dwells."

24. (a) God is eternal and is not bound by time. Peter describes this to us by stating that a thousand years and a single day are equivalent to Him. (b) The final judgment has not yet come because God, in His mercy, wants to give people a chance for repentance.

25. (a) We will be like Him. (b) Clearly, there is nothing better for which we could ever hope.

Signs of the Times

Matthew 24:3–28

Preparing for the Session

Central Focus

The main purpose of this lesson is to familiarize the student with the signs that the Bible gives to remind us that Christ will really come back to judge the living and the dead. These signs occur in nature, society, and the Church. Many people—including church people—refuse to believe that the world will end the way the Bible says, but the signs say otherwise. People need to be ready.

Objectives

That participants, led by the Holy Spirit working through God's Word, will

1. learn about the signs of the end times that Jesus described to His disciples;

2. learn about the signs that are described elsewhere in the New Testament other than the Gospels; and

3. appreciate God's goodness in providing such signs so as to keep believers' faith focused on the promises associated with the second coming of Jesus.

For the Small-Group Leader

Small-Group Discussion Helps

Day 1 • Matthew 24:1–3; 26:3–5; 23:37–39

1. (a) Jesus told the disciples that the temple would be completely destroyed. They wanted to know when it would happen and what would be the sign of Jesus' second coming. (b) They seemed to link together the destruction of Jerusalem and the second coming. (c) Answers will vary. One possibility is that the disciples viewed the temple as a necessary sign of God's presence with His people.

2. (a) They plotted to arrest Jesus and kill Him. (b) They were afraid of the people.

3. (a) Jesus lamented over how the city had killed the prophets and refused Jesus. They were about to join in the killing of Jesus. (b) As a result, the city would be destroyed—its house would be left "desolate." The Romans destroyed Jerusalem in AD 70.

4. **Challenge question.** Answers will vary. One answer would be that those who receive God's blessings are liable to God's punishment when they are ungrateful and live wickedly.

Day 2 • Matthew 24:4–14, 21–24, 29–31; 7:15–16; Acts 4:8–12; 23:28–29; 2 Corinthians 4:17

5. (a) The first sign was the coming of false christs. They would attempt to lead Christians astray; that is, away from Christ to false beliefs. (b) We are warned not to trust in the performance of great signs and wonders.

6. Since the job of a true prophet is to speak the Word of God, a false prophet is someone who passes off false doctrine in the name of the Lord. See Jeremiah 23:31. The Scriptures help us recognize what is true and false in their teachings.

7. Signs in nature include famines and earthquakes; signs in the affairs of nations are wars and rumors of wars; nation against nation, kingdom against kingdom. All such will come to an end, because God will end sin and its consequences.

8. Persecution and the apostasy (falling away) has been going on from the earliest days of the Church. Just think of Stephen, Peter, and Paul from the Book of Acts (6:12; 12:3; and 14:19). Christ has promised to cut short the days of tribulation for the sake of the elect.

9. (a) "This gospel of the kingdom will be proclaimed throughout the whole world" (Matthew 24:14). (b) This clearly demonstrates to us that God wants to save people, not damn them.

Day 3 • Matthew 24:36; 1 Thessalonians 5:2; 2 Peter 3:10; Revelation 3:3; Matthew 24:38–41

10. (a) The signs are continual reminders to us that the world will end and that Christ will come back. (b) They do not indicate when that will take place.

11. (a) "But concerning that day and hour no one knows" (Matthew 24:36). (b) Answers will vary. One possibility is that we would be tempted to live in sin right up until the last moment, planning to repent just before the end comes.

12. The expression "a thief in the night" teaches us to be ready at all times, for the end will come when people are not expecting it.

13. (a) People will be going about their normal activities like eating and drinking, marrying and giving in marriage. (b) The people of Noah's day were completely unprepared for the end. They did not use the time prior to the flood for repentance. Jesus does not want that to happen to us.

14. (a) Answers will vary, but a good answer might be "Be prepared!" (b) Judgment Day is the climactic moment for every person. Only those who repent are truly prepared. We need to take advantage of the time now to prepare ourselves and to preach to others.

Day 4 • 1 Thessalonians 5:1–10; 2 Thessalonians 1:5–10; 2:1–12; 1 John 2:18; 4:3

15. "There is peace and security," they will say. Paul contrasts people of darkness with children of light. The former sleep and get drunk; the latter are awake, sober, and ready.

16. The main idea behind this passage is that a Christian is ready for the end whenever it comes by remaining true to the faith, by exercising love toward all, and by continuing to hope in Jesus' promises. Paul uses the idea of armor in other places besides here (e.g., Ephesians 6:11–17). He also mentions faith, love, and hope as three chief Christian virtues in other places as well (e.g., 1 Corinthians 13:13).

17. (a) They will suffer God's wrath instead of receiving salvation. (b) This will happen because they belong to darkness, that is, they remain under the domination of sin and Satan. (c) God is certainly not being unfair. God's justice remains in force against those who refuse to repent and believe the Gospel.

18. The man of lawlessness exalts himself over all gods and religions. In fact, he claims to be God. He sits in the temple of God. He is "lawless"; that is, he acts and teaches contrary to the Word of God and so brings destruction upon all who follow him.

19. (a) "Antichrist." (b) The pope claimed to be the head of the Church on earth and to speak with the authority of Christ Himself, but he spoke contrary to Christ and denied salvation by faith in Christ alone. Instead, he taught that one could achieve salvation only by subservience to the pope and by doing the works that the "Church" prescribed.

Day 5 • Revelation 20; Matthew 25:31–32; Acts 2:17

20. They believe that Christ will reign for one thousand years upon the earth before the Last Day.

21. This chapter refers to an angel with "the key to the bottomless pit"; calls Satan a "dragon" whom an angel locks in the pit; talks about worshiping "the beast"; mentions the "mark" of the beast that one finds on foreheads or hands; and describes the devil, Death, and Hades as being thrown into "the lake of fire." All of this is symbolic language (just like the reference to a millennium) that must be interpreted.

22. (a) In Revelation 1:13–16, Jesus' hair was as white as wool or snow; His eyes were like flames; His feet were like burnished bronze; His voice sounded like the roaring of rushing water; and His face shone like the sun. In His right hand, He held seven stars, and a sword protruded from His mouth. (b) In Revelation 5:5, He is called the Lion of Judah, the Root of David. (c) In Revelation 5:6, He is described as a lamb—one that has been slain—with seven horns and seven eyes. (d) No.

23. (a) Christ tells us that He will sit on His glorious throne and judge humanity. (b) He will not set up an earthly kingdom.

24. (a) Peter indicated that the "last days" were beginning on Pentecost. (b) The signs continue throughout the history of the Church—famines, earthquakes, wars, and persecution. Thus, we are always in the "last days." God has accomplished everything for our salvation. We are waiting for just one thing: the return of Jesus.

So What?

Matthew 24:42–44

Preparing for the Session

Central Focus

The goal of this lesson is to draw out implications for the Christian life from the doctrine of the end times. In particular, this lesson shows that the second coming provides a powerful incentive to remain in the faith and to serve God by serving others. God's promises of life everlasting and resurrection also offer great encouragement to believers when they must experience troubles here.

Objectives

That participants, led by the Holy Spirit working through God's Word, will

1. understand that the doctrine of the end times has direct implications for their faith and life;

2. learn what the Bible has to say about the Christian life in view of the end; and

3. find comfort when they face death in the promises of Christ for believers at the end of time.

For the Small-Group Leader

Small-Group Discussion Helps

Day 1 • Matthew 24:42–44; 10:22; Revelation 2:10; Matthew 24:22, 29–31; Ephesians 1:4–5; Acts 7:60

1. Christians should "stay awake"; that is, be ready at all times for His return.

2. (a) Answers will vary, but the examples will probably fall into these categories: persecution, tribulation, and temptation. (b) "The crown of life."

3. This word brings all the comfort in the world. Salvation does not rest in our puny abilities but in the all-powerful hands of a loving God. As Jesus said, "You did not choose Me, but I chose you" (John 15:16).

4. (a) God loved you from before the foundation of the world; that is, from all eternity. (b) Answers will vary. They might include infant Baptism, Christian home, parochial school, Christian charity, or witnessing by others.

5. (a) Times of persecution or tribulation can always be recognized as times of Jesus' return. God will not abandon His people, but He will return to deliver them. (b) Persecution can become very intense and can even include martyrdom.

Day 2 • 2 Peter 3:1–13

6. (a) Everything seems just the way it was since the beginning of time. They are following their own sinful desires. (b) Answers will vary, but clearly, they are letting their sinful desires get in the way of seeing the signs. They don't want there to be judgment because if there is, they might have to change their ways in anticipation of that judgment.

7. (a) They are forgetting the creation and the flood, both of which occurred only on account of God's Word. Without that Word, nothing would have happened. (b) God's Word is also what tells us that the end will come and that the world will be destroyed by fire. That Word is absolutely true and we can (must!) rely on it.

8. (a) God wants all to reach repentance. He is patient toward sinful mankind. (b) Although no Christian likes waiting, God's patience is testimony to His mercy toward humanity in Jesus. Ultimately, this is comforting.

9. God will create new heavens and a new earth in which righteousness dwells.

10. Since we know by the assurance of God's Word not only that judgment but also that a new and wonderful creation is coming, we should be motivated to live the way God wants us to, in faith, love, and hope.

Day 3 • Matthew 13:47–50; 13:24–30, 36–43; 24:32–35

11. The parable teaches us that Judgment Day is certainly coming and that God will employ the angels to carry it out. The angels will commit the unbelievers to hell.

12. (a) The master tells his servants not to pull the weeds lest they pull up some wheat with the weeds. (b) This represents our Lord's patience—as we have seen in

2 Peter 3:9, He does not want people to perish, so He is giving the world time for repentance.

13. (a) The harvest in the parable represents the close of the age and final judgment. The Son of Man will send forth His angels to gather up all causes of sin and all law-breakers and hurl them into hell. (b) As bad as it seems, this is not permanent. While there is time, some may repent; but at the end, Christ will come and condemn the wicked.

14. (a) Just as we know that summer is almost here when we see a tree begin to put out its leaves, so when we see the signs of the times that Jesus has described, we should know that the end is near. We should call people's attention to these signs and remind them that the end is coming. (b) We should patiently endure all trials and live by faith and repentance, but we should also make use of the time to evangelize the world because time is running out.

15. Answers will vary. One good reason for parables is that they are memorable. We can more easily recall the truth when Christ has conveyed it by a story.

Day 4 • Matthew 25:1–13; 24:45–51; 25:14–30; Galatians 5:14

16. (a) We need always to be ready for Judgment Day. We know that it is coming, but we don't know when. (b) Since the bridegroom was late, the five foolish virgins ran out of oil and of time to get more. They missed the wedding feast. But the wise virgins who had planned ahead were ready when they bridegroom arrived, so they entered the feast.

17. (a) Christ, who has promised to return. (b) Believers who remain faithful until the end. (c) One-time believers who fall away because of temptation or persecution. They deceive themselves into thinking that Christ is never going to come back. (d) That which is essential to salvation. Faith in Christ is probably the best answer. But perhaps one could say good works; that is, the necessary fruit of faith.

18. The faithful servant carries out the duties entrusted to him by his master, especially that of providing food for the household at the right time. The wicked servant spends his time in carousing and beating his fellow servants. Christians live the way God wants them to, especially by serving their neighbor in love.

19. (a) The final command of the master to cast the third servant into "outer darkness" where "there will be weeping and gnashing of teeth" (Matthew 25:30) depicts Judgment Day. (b) God gives gifts of all kinds to His people and expects each one to use these gifts in the service of God. As Paul has summarized it, "You shall love your neighbor as yourself" (Galatians 5:14), or again, "Let us do good to everyone, and especially to those who are of the household of faith" (Galatians 6:10). But those who fail to do so, God will condemn.

20. (a) Answers will vary. They will include both temporal and spiritual blessings. (b) Love is the center of Christian living.

Day 5 • Philippians 3:21; 1 Thessalonians 4:16–18; Hebrews 2:14–15; Romans 6:3–4; 1 Corinthians 15:20, 53–57

21. We look forward to Jesus transforming our lowly bodies to be like His glorious one.

22. Death often involves much ugliness, uncertainty, and suffering, painful for both the dying and the survivors. We find comfort in the glorious return of Christ and the resurrection of the believing dead to greet Him.

23. (a) The one who has power over death (as the punishment for sin) is the devil. However, Jesus became a true human being. This made it possible for Him to die in our place and then, by rising, to destroy the power of death and devil over humanity. (b) Answers will vary. Certainly, they will include both what Jesus has done for us and what He will do for us at death and the end of time.

24. (a) We are buried with Christ by Baptism. (b) We no longer have to fear death as punishment for sin but can accept it as the entrance into heaven.